LITTLE BADGER

KNITWEAR

LITTLE BADGER

KNITWEAR

Knitted projects for babies and toddlers

Ros Badger and Elaine Scott

Photographs by Ben Murphy

The Taunton Press

First published in 2000

1 3 5 7 9 10 8 6 4 2

Text and knitwear designs © Ros Badger and
Elaine Scott, 2000
Photographs © Ben Murphy, 2000

Photographer: Ben Murphy
Stylist: Ros Badger
Designer: Lawrence Morton
Illustrator: Anthony Duke

Taunton
BOOKS & VIDEOS

for fellow enthusiasts

First published in the United Kingdom in 2000
by Ebury Press, Random House,
20 Vauxhall Bridge Road, London SW1V 2SA

The Taunton Press, Inc.
63 South Main St.
PO Box 5506
Newtown, CT 06470-5506
www.taunton.com

Distributed by Publishers Group West

Library of Congress Cataloging-in-
Publication Data

Badger, Ros.
    Little Badger Knitwear: Knitted
    projects for babies and toddlers/
    Ros Badger and Elaine Scott.
    p. cm.
    ISBN 1-56158-414-2
    1. Knitting–Patterns. 2. Children's
    clothing. I. Scott, Elaine. II. Title.
TT825. B294 2000
746.43'20432–dc21 99-086090

Printed and bound in Singapore

Contents

Introduction

Elaine Scott and I launched the first Little Badger mail order catalogue in spring 1996, specializing in children's handmade knitwear. I had already worked successfully for a number of years as a freelance knitwear designer with many top names in the fashion industry, including Betty Jackson, Flyte Ostell and Duffer of St. George. Elaine had run a knitwear company in the 1980s with her sister (who now does some of Little Badger's production), and had later worked as an accounts manager for other fashion companies. We had both stopped working at roughly the same time, when our first children were born. I began to knit clothes for my daughter, Martha, and quickly realized through people's reactions that there was a demand for well-made, stylish children's handknits. Elaine and I both wanted to start a business and, after a chance meeting through friends, decided to pool our experiences. We now find ourselves with a growing business.

Our design influences range from contemporary fashion trends to original knitting patterns from the thirties, forties and fifties. We planned from the outset to use only the best quality natural materials. With this book, you can now knit some of our favourite classic designs using updated traditional knitting techniques and a modern colour palette. The knitting ability for each style varies from very easy to difficult, so there are challenges here for all levels of home knitter. Whatever you favour, from a funky pirate sweater to a smart heart hat or classic cable sweater – we know you will find something that you love in this book.

Ros Badger and Elaine Scott

Denim coat dress

When Rowan first brought out their denim cotton yarn in the 1980s, I bought some straight away. I really liked the way it is designed to fade with washing and thought it would be a really interesting yarn to work with, but then I couldn't think what to do with it so it just sat on a shelf gathering dust. A few years later, when I was pregnant with my first daughter Martha, I was looking through some old knitting patterns as my mother had offered to knit some clothes for the baby. I found some lovely old-fashioned pram coats which provided the inspiration for this Denim coat dress. I used the denim cotton yarn with coconut shell buttons, and updated the traditional pram coat design by using moss stitch edging instead of lace, to create a coat dress that looks just a good with pretty dresses or dungarees as it does with a Christening robe.

My second daughter Ceidra still wears the original Denim coat dress which is now very washed out and faded, just like a much-loved pair of jeans, but still looks great.

Pattern on page 58

Denim leggings, mitts and booties

Like the Denim coat dress, the original Denim leggings, mitts and booties were made by my mother for Martha when she was a baby. I based these designs on an old baby layette pattern I had come across, using the basic shapes for the garments but taking away any unnecessary fussiness so they were not too pretty and more suited to knitting in 4-ply yarn. Instead of using the usual elastic for the waist of the leggings, I made a twisted cord from the denim cotton yarn to give a more quirky look. However, if for ease of dressing you prefer elastic then by all means use that instead of the cord. All these designs could be knitted in any 4-ply yarn, and the look of each will vary depending on the colours chosen. I particularly love the effect of the denim cotton yarn, especially the way wear on the knees and bottom of the leggings really shows as the yarn fades. The Denim mittens and booties on their own make a lovely gift for a newborn baby as people really appreciate the special effort that goes into a handmade present.

Patterns on pages 59–60

Quaker ridge cardigan

I came across the Quaker ridge stitch many years ago in an old American knitting stitches book. I first used it for a woman's waistcoat I designed when working with British designer Betty Jackson. In this original design I used six different shades of a linen slub for the stripes and one contrast colour for the garter stitch ridges. Here, in this children's cardigan, I have used just two shades of denim cotton yarn but this design would work equally well in multi-colours giving a rainbow effect instead of the more subtle denim stripes. Even using three colours, such as navy and cream stripes with red ridges, would give this garment a completely different look to the one shown here. It is always worth adding your own influences when knitting to make your work a complete one off.

Pattern on pages 60–1

Cot blanket

Shaker designs, patchwork blankets and antique quilts all
provided the initial inspiration for this Cot blanket. I have
always liked the faded colours of old-fashioned quilts, and
have tried to achieve the same look with this Cot blanket by
using slightly washed-out colours. I have included both a
baby blue and a rose pink in this blanket, however, as I want
it to appeal to parents of both boys and girls alike. The idea
for embroidering the name and date of birth of the child at
the top and bottom of the blanket is taken from traditional
samplers, where the embroiderer would add their own name
to their work. A fellow knitter once gave me a pair of socks
knitted at the end of the nineteenth century. These socks
were so fine they looked as though they had been knitted on
the smallest pins, and each had the maker's initials knitted
in. This kind of archive material always inspires me, and I
try to recreate the same attention to detail in my own work.

Pattern on pages 61–3

Ballet cardigan

When Matilda was three years old her passion for dressing up led her to ballet classes, so Elaine found a local school for her to attend once a week. My daughter Martha quickly caught on to this idea and, as soon as she was old enough, joined Matilda in the dance class. I was immediately obliged to buy exactly the right leotard and net skirt, but I just could not bring myself to buy the cardigan. It was a sickly shade of pink and mass produced in acrylic – not my favourite type of yarn! I could see that I was not the only mother to prefer a garment made of natural yarn, that fitted properly and could be worn with other clothes. So the ballet cardigan was born and, if our mail orders are anything to go by, it seems to have been gratefully received. It works well in a variety of colours and can double as a party cardigan if your little angel is not a ballerina.

Pattern on page 64

Square-neck cardigan

When I saw a square-necked, silk jersey vest in a museum, I immediately thought the simple neck detail would work really well on a baby cardigan. In this design, I have used my favourite moss stitch to emphasize the square shape of the neck, button bands and hems. This Square-necked cardigan is quite a simple garment to make as there are no extra pieces to attach, so it's a good design for an inexperienced knitter.

Pattern on page 65

Museum sweater

In one of the many knitting books I have collected over the years from charity shops and flea markets I found the stitch pattern which inspired this sweater. Combined with the basic shape of a grandad vest and knitted in denim cotton yarn, I have created a simple baby sweater with an slightly old-fashioned feel. When the original Museum sweater was finished and washed, it emerged from the laundry much smaller than I had anticipated and the denim had already started to fade. It occurred to me that this sweater wouldn't look out of place in a museum display of nineteenth-century workers' clothing, so hence its name.

The original sweater has been worn by both my daughters and a number of friends' babies too, but it is now safely back with me where I think it will stay as a reminder of just how small newborn babies are.

Pattern on page 66

Quaker ridge pixie hat

Most old children's knitting patterns include a hat to match the sweater. This is an idea that really appeals to me, especially for babies and toddlers as it is so important to keep their heads warm in winter. So, having finished the Quaker ridge cardigan, I set to work on this matching hat. The rings of garter stitch look great as they reduce in size up the hat, then it flops over with a large tassle on the end to make a lovely pixie hat.

Pattern on page 67

Crossover-back sweater

As well as old knitting patterns, I collect antique knitwear
and have an archive box that I often delve into to spark
ideas. In this box is a moth-eaten baby sweater I bought in
a flea market simply because I like the way it fastened at
the back. I had not seen this kind of back fastening before,
but realized that it is very convenient for babies as it makes
the sweater easy to put on and take off. I have based this
Crossover-back sweater around that detail, added subtle
decoration to the front and sleeves by using my trademark
heart motif and moss stitch, and created one of my
favourite baby garments.

Pattern on page 68

Dragon hat

I have had to learn quite quickly how much children like to make-believe. As Martha, my oldest daughter, is particularly into dressing-up I decided to incorporate some of her fairy-tale ideas into my knitwear. She especially loves fairies, pixies and angels, but there is always a 'baddie' involved as well, whether it be a wicked queen or a sea witch. So it seemed exciting for her to be able to pull on a hat and become a different character. I particularly like the tail on this hat. It is an unexpected detail that adds to its individuality. The fact that this hat can be cute or a bit scary makes it very appealing to children.

Pattern on page 69

Pirate sweater

During the 1980s I designed a series of sweaters for a shop called Johnson's LA Rocka on London's Kings Road. The theme for this collection was bikers and rock and roll, and one of my favourite designs was always a skull and crossbones sweater. In 1991, when a friend of mine had twin girls, Mia and Rosa, her sister Celia asked if I could make two miniature versions of this sweater for a present. They worked really well and everyone loved them so, when we set up Little Badger five years later, the renamed Pirate sweater was the first sample made. It has remained in our catalogue ever since.

Pattern on pages 70–1

Sunflower sweater

Whilst on holiday one summer in Tuscany, I saw field upon field of huge sunflowers and thought this would be a lovely image to try to knit. When I got back home, I chose some colours that I felt captured those hot, sunny days and worked them into this design. The frill edge which hems this sweater looks like the petals of a flower, however, as this is knitted separately, you could just as easily leave a plain garter stitch edge, if preferred. This Sunflower sweater has been a consistently popular style in our catalogues. Instead of ecru, I have also tried it with a navy background which gives it a more autumnal feel but is equally as pretty.

Pattern on pages 72–3

Starfish jacket

Whilst on holiday in Cornwall a few years ago, my
daughter Martha was playing in some rock pools with her
friends, Daisy and Alabama. They were finding all sorts of
treasures in their fishing nets. The way the clear water and
sunshine intensified the colours and lustre of the seashells
and starfish inspired the decoration of this jacket. When I
got home, I began working on a new children's collection
and used my holiday memories as inspiration for this
Starfish jacket.

Pattern on pages 74–7

Heart sweater

This is an adaptation of the original Heart sweater included in the very first Little Badger catalogue, and it is still one of my favourite designs. I initially designed this sweater for a shop called The Cross in London's Holland Park. For the first year they stocked it in light denim with a dark denim heart motif, which was a very successful colourway and would be worth trying as a variation to the pink cotton and red chenille shown here. The texture of the chenille on the matt cotton is a lovely effect, however, and most children like the velvety feel of the heart. I have also tried knitting it completely in DK cotton which works very well, so if you can't find chenille don't be put off – use the opportunity to experiment. You could even try using wool and mohair together to give a similar textured effect.

Pattern on pages 78–9

Soccer sweater

As the World Cup was about to start in France, Vanessa, our sports-mad assistant, thought a Soccer sweater might be a popular design for our spring 1998 catalogue. I set to work on the design. It took quite a while to work out a proper knitted circle, and I have to admit there were a few rugby ball shapes among the first samples! I then had to tackle the pentagon-shaped patches of a traditional black and white football. This was quite a challenge, but I am really pleased with the finished result. Instead of using the colours shown here, you could knit the background in the colours of your favourite team and keep the football black and white. You could even knit the number of your favourite player on the back of this sweater, then imagine yourself scoring that winning goal.

Pattern on pages 80–1

Star sweater

After seeing the Heart sweater, my friends with boy babies
felt they needed a version for their sons, and the star
design was the obvious choice. I have now made a number
of variations on this design simply by changing yarns and
colours. If you don't like the seaside feel of the navy and
ecru cotton version shown here, try knitting the sweater in
navy with a gold chenille star to give a Christmas feel. The
original gold Star sweater was made for Matthew Stone
when he was just nine months old. Matthew has now
outgrown the sweater, but it has since been passed down to
his younger sister Mair.

Pattern on pages 82–3

Popeye sweater

I see the Popeye sweater as little brother to the Pirate
sweater. I wanted to design another boy's style (although it
looks great on girls too), and decided to continue the biker
theme. The idea for the anchor came from pictures of
sailors, tattoos and also the cartoon character Popeye,
hence the name of the sweater. Originally, the Popeye
sweater had a heart on the sleeve as well, but I have tamed
it down here making it easier to knit. This sweater looks
great on children when worn with jeans and boots but, as
with all the designs in this book, you could easily change
the background colour of this sweater to give it a
completely different look.

Pattern on pages 84–5

Sherlock hat

A few years ago I designed a small range of crotchet accessories for British designer Margaret Howell. There were a few of the smaller sized hats left over, so I decided to customise them. I very much like the texture of double crotchet; it is neat and comfortable to wear, a necessity when making hats for children. By unpicking the original hat a little, I found it made a perfect skull-cap shape. I then added earflaps to the hat to keep out the wind and the ties to keep it securely on the head. I have called it a Sherlock hat as it reminds me of an old deerstalker.

Pattern on page 86

Zig-zag sweater

I used to design my own range of men's knitwear, which included a sweater very similar to this one. It was always very popular with adults, so I have adapted the design for children. I love the combination of cables and moss stitch which form this Zag-zag sweater: the cables lend a traditional touch, but the look of this sweater can really vary depending on what it's combined with. Here it has been teamed with a lace skirt, showing just how adaptable it can be. In the past, I have also knitted this pattern in wool instead of cotton yarn which completely changes the look of this sweater.

Pattern on pages 86–7

Star jacket

The basic shape of this Star jacket came from a 1950s
men's knitted jacket I bought about ten years ago in an
antique clothes shop in Edinburgh. This style of jacket
usually has a zip in the front, but for this children's version
I have replaced the zip with buttons. I have used garter
stitch for the button band and shawl collar to keep that
1950's feel. I especially like the way this jacket looks quite
classic from the front but is given a contemporary twist by
the star motif on the back.

Pattern on pages 88–9

Heart and Star hats and scarves

The success of the Heart and Star sweaters inevitably led on to these hats and scarves. I have designed lots of knitted hats but this 'beanie' is one of the simplest shapes to make. This basic shape is so simple to knit that even the least experienced knitter could knit a plain hat in an evening.

The scarf is equally simple to make. Vanessa, our assistant, used to have her own scarf company, and came up with the idea for this design. There is a vertical split at the end of the scarf through which the opposite end is threaded, making sure you can see the heart or star whilst being just as secure as a knot.

Pattern on pages 90–1

Heart and Star rucksacks

My daughter Martha and Elaine's daughter Matilda both seem to collect countless bags. They particularly like rucksacks as it means their hands are free to search out all the treasures which fill up their bags. A knitted rucksack that matches the popular Heart and Star sweaters seemed the perfect choice as they are strong images which look good from a distance as well as feel fantastic close up. I really like the finished results, and so do all their friends, including the boys!

Pattern on pages 92–3

patterns

Basic information

Sizes

Where instructions are given for more than one size, the figures for the larger sizes are given in round () brackets whilst the smallest size is given outside the brackets. Where only one figures appears, this figure applies to all sizes and where 0 appears no stitches or rows are worked for this size. Where figures are given in square [] brackets, work these figures the number of times stated after the brackets.

Sizes are given in ages and are intended as an average guide only, although approximate body width, body length and sleeve length measurements are given in the table below. Our patterns tend to err on the generous side but, as children of similar ages can vary so much, use your tension swatch to establish which size is best for your child.

Age	body width	body length	centre back to cuff
0–6 months	24 cm	24 cm	29 cm
6–12 months	28 cm	29 cm	35 cm
1–2 years	32 cm	34 cm	45 cm
2–4 years	37 cm	41 cm	49 cm
4–6 years	41 cm	46 cm	55 cm

Yarns

I have recommended a yarn type for each pattern and estimated the quantity each should take. All quantities are given to the nearest 50g. I have been quite generous when estimating the yarn quantities as I know how irritating it is to run out of yarn with just a few rows left to finish the garment.

If you cannot find the particular yarn specified in the pattern, any other make of yarn that is the same type and weight should work just as well, but you must always work a tension swatch before beginning a garment and change the needles you are using accordingly to achieve the correct tension.

If you do substitute the suggested yarn for a different make, check the metredge on the ball band as, even though they may weigh the same, yarns can vary greatly in length. If you are unsure when choosing a substitute yarn for a garment, ask the assistant at your yarn shop for advice.

The following descriptions of the various Dyed in the Wool, Jaeger, Rowan and Little Badger yarns are meant as a guide to the yarn type (ie. cotton, chenille, wool, etc) and weight.

Dyed in the Wool Cotton Chenille: a double knitting-weight cotton chenille yarn (100% cotton); approximately 70 m per 50 g/1¾ oz ball.

Jaeger Pure Cotton: a double knitting-weight cotton yarn (100% cotton); approximately 112 m per 50 g/1¾ oz ball.

Jaeger Siena: a 4-ply-weight mercerised cotton yarn (100% cotton); approximately 140 m per 50 g/1¾ oz ball.

Rowan Designer DK: a double knitting-weight wool yarn (100% wool); approximately 115 m per 50 g/1¾ oz ball.

Rowan DK Soft: a double knitting-weight wool yarn (85% wool; 15% polyamide); approximately 175 m per 50 g/1¾ oz ball.

Rowan Fine Cotton Chenille: a double knitting-weight cotton yarn (89% cotton; 11% polyester); approximately 160 m per 50 g/1¾ oz ball.

Rowan Handknit DK Cotton: a double knitting-weight cotton yarn (100% cotton); approximately 85 m per 50 g/1¾ oz ball.

Rowan 4-Ply Cotton: a 4 ply-weight cotton yarn (100% cotton); approximately 170 m per 50 g/1¾ oz ball.

Denim 4-Ply Cotton (available by mail order from Little Badger): a 4ply-weight cotton yarn (100% cotton); approximately 180 m per 50 g/1¾ oz ball.

In the US, balls or hanks of yarn are sold in ounces, not in grams; the weights of the relevant Dyed in the Wool, Jaeger, Rowan and Little Badger yarns are given above.

Addresses for suppliers of all the yarns listed below can be found on pages 94–5 on this book.

Tension

Tension is the number of stitches and rows per centimetre that should be obtained on the given needles, yarn and stitch pattern. Achieving the correct tension is very important when making children's clothing as it determines the finished size of the garment. A tension is specified for each pattern in this book, so always work a tension swatch before beginning a garment.

To check your tension, work a sample at least 10 cm square using the given yarn, needles and stitch pattern used for the garment. Press the tension swatch lightly on a flat surface, but do not stretch the sample. Using a ruler, measure and mark the number of stitches and rows in the central area of the sample and check this number against the set tension. If you have too many stitches try another swatch using larger needles, but if you have too few stitches try again with smaller needles.

Ability

Patterns are graded from 1 to 5 according to difficulty. Patterns rated 1 are the easiest, and are suitable for beginners, whilst patterns rated 5 are the most difficult and require some experience.

Abbreviations

A few specific knitting terms are used in this book and may be unfamiliar to some readers. The list below explains the abbreviations used in the patterns.

alt = alternate
beg = begin(ning)
cm = centimetre
cn = cable needle
cont = continue
dc = double crotchet
dec = decreas(e)ing
foll = following
folls = follows
gt st = garter st (knit every row)
inc = increas(e)ing
k = knit
lh = left hand needle
m1 = make one (pick up horizontal loop before
  next st and work into back of it)
ms st = moss st (row 1: k1, p1, rep to end; row 2: p1, k1,
  rep to end)
patt = pattern
p = purl
psso = pass slipped stitch over
rem = remain(ing)
rep = repeat
rh = right hand needle
rs = right side
rev = reversing
skpo = slip 1, knit 1, pass slipped stitch over
sl = slip
sl st = slip stitch
st(s) = stitch(es)
st st = stocking stitch (knit 1 row, purl 1 row)
tbl = through back of loop
tog = together
ws = wrong side
yb = yarn back
yf = yarn forward
yon = yarn over needle
yrn = yarn round needle

Ribs and edges

All ribs and edges should be knitted firmly to give a good finish to your garment. If your ribs and edges are a little too slack, change to smaller needles for a firmer tension.

Charts

Each square depicted on the charts represents one stitch and each line of squares represents one row. Stitches depicted on the charts are all worked in stocking stitch unless otherwise stated. When reading from a chart start at the bottom right-hand corner unless otherwise stated and read from right to left for right-side rows and left to right for wrong-side rows. Each stitch and/or colour used is given a symbol in the key, so check the key to the chart before beginning a pattern.

Intarsia

Intarsia is one of the main methods of working colour into knitted garments. The easiest way to work intarsia is to wind off small lengths of yarn for each coloured area to be worked.

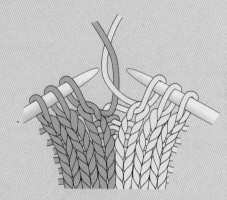

When knitting, link one yarn to the next by twisting the two yarns around each other once at the change over point on the wrong side of the work. This will avoid gaps. All ends should then be darned in along the colour join lines. Never weave into a row as this will show through to the right side. Be particularly careful to keep an even tension.

Chenille

Chenille does not have the same elasticity as other yarns, so the stitches need to kept close together. When knitting with chenille try to keep each stitch worked at the tip of the right hand needle and work the next stitch as close to it as possible to maintain a good tension. Chenille also has a pile which, for the best results, should run away from your knitting rather than towards it. Run your fingers down the yarn to feel the direction of the pile – it should feel smoother running in one direction than the other – and make sure this pile runs away from your work when knitting. Always use bamboo needles for knitting with chenille as the stitches run more smoothly than on metal needles.

Denim cotton

Denim cotton yarn dyed with real indigo dye possess many of the same qualities of denim jeans. It will shrink on its initial wash and continue to fade with repeated wearing and washes. The dye loss will be greatest during the initial wash, so be careful to wash the garment separately. The garment will shrink by approximately 20% in length when first washed but the width will remain the same, so the garment will seem a little long whilst knitting. All measurements given in the patterns are before washing, before shrinkage has taken place.

Finishing and pressing

The finish of a garment can often let the work down if it is not done properly. After putting so many loving hours into your knitting, try to put the pieces together with just as much care. Press the work with a good steam iron or press over a damp cloth, but do not press the garment out of shape or flatten the texture. Be very careful not to press ribs so that they stretch out of shape. When sewing up, I prefer to use mattress stitch for most seams although I sometimes use backstitch to sew in sleeves. Never overstitch when making up a garment as this makes for a very bulky finish.

Mattress stitch

This is the best stitch to use for an invisible seam when making up garments as it provides a really neat finish. With right sides face up, lay the two pieces of knitting to be joined together side by side.

Bring the yarn needle through to the front of the right-hand piece and insert it between the edge stitch and second stitch on the first two rows. Then take the yarn needle across and pick up the corresponding two strands between the edge stitch and second stitch on the first and second rows of the left-hand piece. Repeat this zig-zag action back and forth until the pieces are joined all the way along. Pull the yarn to join the seam, pulling it a little tighter than necessary at first, then stretch the seam back into shape.

Backstitch

This stitch provides a good strong seam. With right sides together, hold the two pieces of knitting to be joined in one hand.

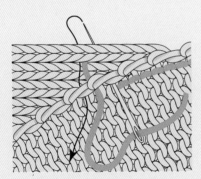

Insert the yarn needle up between the edge stitch and second stitch between the first and second row. Pull the yarn tight. Insert the yarn needle down between the first row and cast-on edge, then up between the second and third row. Pull the yarn tight. Continue always going down where you first went up, and up one row further along.

Caring for your garment

Check the ball band of your yarn for the washing instructions. If you are handwashing, wrap the garment in a towel after washing to get rid of any excess moisture. Reshape the garment and dry flat away from a direct heat.

UK and US terms

The following terms may be unfamiliar to US readers:

UK terms	US terms
ball band	yarn wrapper
cast off	bind off
DK wool	knitting worsted yarn
double crotchet	single crotchet
make up (garment)	finish (garment)
mattress stitch	ladder stitch
rib	ribbing
stocking stitch	stockinette stitch
tension	gauge
yarn forward	yarn over

UK and US needle sizes

2.25 mm	no. 13	US 0
2.5 mm		
2.75 mm	no. 12	US 1
3 mm	no. 11	US 2
3.25 mm	no. 10	US 3
3.5 mm		
3.75 mm	no. 9	US 4
4 mm	no. 8	US 5
4.5 mm	no. 7	US 6

Denim coat dress

See picture on page 9

<u>Size</u> To fit age 0–6 months; 6–12 months
<u>Yarn</u> 4 (4) x 50 g balls of 4-Ply Denim Cotton in light or dark denim (available by mail order from Little Badger) or 4 (4) x 50 g balls of Rowan 4-Ply Cotton
<u>Needles</u> 1 pair each of 2.75 mm (no. 12/US 2) and 3.25 mm (no. 10/US 3)

<u>Tension</u> 35 sts and 50 rows to 10 cm square over st st on 3.25 mm (no. 10/ US 3) needles after washing. Always work a tension swatch and change needles accordingly if necessary (see Basic Information, page 54).
<u>Ability</u> 3
<u>Abbreviations</u> See Basic Information, pages 54–6.
<u>Note</u> Denim yarn shrinks approximately 20% after washing, so this garment may seem a little long when knitting. Always dec or inc using fully-fashioned method (i.e. on 3rd stitch from row edge).

Back

With 3.25 mm (no. 10/US 3) needles, cast on 107 (121) sts. Work 5 rows in ms st. Cont in st st until Back measures 20 (24) cm from cast-on edge if using denim cotton or 17 (20) cm if using plain cotton, ending with a p row. Change to 2.75 mm (no. 12/US 2) needles. K 1 row.

Shape waist

Next row [p2tog] 7 times, [p1, p2tog] 24 (31) times, [p2tog] 7 times.
Change to 3.25 mm (no. 10/US 3) needles. Work 7 rows in ms st. Cont in st st until Back measures 25.5 (29) cm from cast-on edge if using denim cotton or 22.5 (25) cm if using plain cotton, ending with a p row.

Shape armholes

Cast off 4 sts at beg of next 2 rows. Cont in st st, but dec 1 st at each of next row and every foll row until 44 (58) sts rem. Cont in st st until Back measures 34 (38.5) cm from cast-on edge if using denim cotton or 31 (34.5) cm if using plain cotton.

Shape shoulders

Place 12 (17) sts at each end on stitch holder if grafting shoulder seams or cast off. Place rem 20 (24) sts across centre on stitch holder for collar.

Left Front

With 3.25 mm (no. 10/US 3) needles, cast on 59 (67) sts. Work 5 rows in ms st.
Next row k to last 7 sts, work in ms st to end.
Next row work 7 sts in ms st, p to end.
Rep last 2 rows until Left Front measures 20 (24) cm from cast-on edge if using denim cotton or 17 (20) cm if using plain cotton, ending with a p row. Change to 2.75 mm (no. 12/US 2) needles. Work 1 row in st st keeping ms st border.

Shape waist

Next row work 7 sts in ms st, p8, [p2tog] 22 (26) times.
Change to 3.25 mm (no. 10/US 3) needles.

Work 7 rows in ms st. Cont in st st keeping ms st border until Left Front measures 25.5 (29) cm from cast-on edge if using denim cotton or 22.5 (25) cm if using plain cotton, ending with a p row.

Shape armholes

Next row cast off 4 sts, k to last 7 sts, work 7 sts in ms st.
Cont in st st keeping ms st border, but dec 1 st at armhole edge on next row and every foll row until 28 (33) sts. Cont in st st until Left Front measures 34 (38.5) cm from cast-on edge if using denim cotton or 31 (34.5) cm if using plain cotton.

Shape neck

Cast off 7 (9) sts at neck edge on next row. Cont in st st, but dec 1 st at neck edge on next row and every foll row until 12 (17) sts. Work 2 (2) rows in st st. Place rem 12 (17) sts on stitch holder if grafting shoulder seams or cast off.

Right Front

Work as for Left Front but rev all patterning and shaping until ready to beg waist shaping.

Shape waist and make buttonhole

Next row [p2tog] 22 (26) times, p8, work in ms st to end.
Change to 3.25 mm (no. 10/US 3) needles.
Next row work 3 sts in ms st, cast off next 2 sts, work in ms st to end.
Next row work in ms st to last 3 sts, cast on 2 sts over those cast off in previous row, work in ms st to end.
Work 5 rows in ms st. Cont in st st but keeping ms st border, work a further 5 (7) rows or until Right Front measures 25.5 (29) cm from cast-on edge if using denim cotton or 22.5 (25) cm if using plain cotton, ending with a p row.

Shape armhole and make buttonhole

Next row work 3 sts in ms st, cast off next 2 sts, work 2 sts in ms st, k to end.
Next row cast off 4 sts, p to last 5 sts, work 2 sts in ms st, cast on 2 sts over those cast off in previous row, work in ms st to end.

Cont in st st keeping ms st border, but dec 1 st at armhole edge on next row and every foll row until 28 (33) sts and making 2 further buttonholes at intervals of 10 (12) rows.

Shape neck

Cast off 7 (9) sts at beg of next row. Cont in st st, but dec 1 st at neck edge on next row and every foll row until 12 (17) sts. Work 2 rows in st st. Place rem 12 (17) sts on stitch holder if grafting shoulder seams or cast off.

Sleeves

With 3.25 mm (no. 10/US 3) needles, cast on 37 (41) sts. Work 5 rows in ms st. Work 6 cm in st st if using denim cotton and 5 cm if using plain cotton, ending with a k row. Change to 2.75 mm (no. 12/US 2) needles. Work 13 rows in k1, p1 rib. Change to 3.25 mm (no. 10/US 3) needles. Beg with a k row, cont to work in st st, but inc 1 st at each end on next row and every foll 7th (8th) row until 51 (55) sts. Cont in st st until Sleeve measures 24 (26.5) cm from cast-on edge if using denim cotton or 20 (22) cm if using plain cotton. Cont working in st st, but dec 1 st at each end on next row and every foll row until 23 (27) sts. Cast off.

Collar

With 3.25 mm (no. 10/US 3) needles, cast on 90 sts. Work 5 rows in ms st. Work 10 rows in st st keeping border of 5 sts in ms st.
Next row work 5 sts in ms st, k4, * k2tog, k5 *, rep from * to * to last 11 sts, k2tog, k4, work 5 sts in ms st.
Work 5 rows in st st keeping border of 5 sts in ms st.
Next row work 5 sts in ms st, k4, ** k2tog, k4 **, rep from ** to ** to last 10 sts, k2tog, k3, work 5 sts in ms st.
Work 2 rows in st st keeping a border of 5 sts in ms st. Cast off.

Making Up

Wash and dry all garment pieces before

making up, following instructions given on ball band, to allow garment to shrink. Press all pieces (omitting ribbing) on ws using a warm iron over a damp cloth. Graft or sew shoulder seams. Sew side seams of body and sleeve seams. Sew sleeves into body. Turn back cuffs. Sew collar to neck, placing cast-off collar edge to neck edge and ms st collar edges to centre of front ms st borders. Take care not to stretch neck edge. Sew buttons onto Left Front to match buttonholes on Right Front.

Denim leggings

See picture on page 11

<u>Size</u> To fit age 3–9 months
<u>Yarn</u> 3 x 50 g balls of 4-Ply Denim Cotton in light or dark denim (available by mail order from Little Badger)
<u>Needles</u> 1 pair each of 3 mm (no. 11/US 2–3) and 3.25 mm (no. 10/US 3)
<u>Tension</u> 35 sts and 50 rows to 10 cm square over st st on 3.25 mm (no. 10/US 3) needles after washing. Always work a tension swatch and change needles accordingly if necessary (see Basic Information, page 54).
<u>Ability</u> 3
<u>Abbreviations</u> See Basic Information, pages 54–6.
<u>Note</u> Denim yarn shrinks approximately 20% after washing, so garment may seem a little long when knitting. Always dec or inc using fully-fashioned method (i.e. on 3rd stitch from row edge).

Leggings
With 3 mm (no. 11/US 2–3) needles, cast on 141 sts. Work 6 rows in k1, p1 rib.
Next row * rib 2, m1, p2tog *, rep from * to * to end.
Work 5 rows in k1, p1 rib. Change to 3.25 mm (no. 10/US 3) needles. Work 2 rows in st st.
Shape leggings
Row 1 sl1, k 113, turn.
Row 2 p87, turn.
Row 3 k80, turn.
Row 4 p73, turn.
Row 5 k66, turn.
Row 6 p59, turn.
Row 7 k52, turn.
Row 8 p45, turn.
Row 9 k38, turn.
Row 10 p31, turn.
Row 11 k24, turn.
Row 12 p17, turn.
Row 13 k to end.
Row 14 sl1, p to last st, k1.
Row 15 sl1, k68, [inc in next st] twice, k70.
Beg with a p row, cont in st st on rem 143 sts, but inc 1 st on each side of centre st on next row and every foll 6th row until 157 sts. Cont in st st until Leggings measure 20 cm from each edge, ending with a k row.
Next row sl1, p77, p2tog, p76, k1.
Shape legs
Next row sl1, k77, turn.
Cont on these 78 sts only. Work 45 rows in st st. Cont in st st, but dec 1 st at each end on next row and every foll alt row until 34 sts. Work 6 rows in st st. Change to 3 mm (no. 11/US 2–3) needles.
Row 1 k2tog, k1, * p1, k1 *, rep from * to * to last st, k1.
Rows 2, 4 and 6 sl1, ** p1, k1 **, rep from ** to ** to end.
Rows 3 and 5 sl1, k1 ***, p1, k1 ***, rep from *** to *** to last st, k1.
Next row inc in next st, k1, **** p1, k1 ****, rep from **** to **** to last st, k1.
Change to 3.25 mm (no. 10/US 3) needles.
K 2 rows.
Next row sl1, k27, turn.
Next row sl1, k9, turn.
Shape instep
Cont on these 10 sts only. K 21 rows. Break off yarn. With wrong side facing, rejoin yarn to rem 6 sts.
Next row k6, turn.
Next row sl1, k5, pick up and k15 sts evenly along instep, k10, pick up 15 sts along other side of instep, k18.
K 3 rows.
Shape foot
Row 1 sl1, k18, [k2tog] twice, k6, [k2tog] twice, k24, [k2tog] twice, k3.
Rows 2, 4 and 6 k to end.
Row 3 sl1, k17, [k2tog] twice, k4, [k2tog] twice, k22, [k2tog] twice, k2.
Row 5 sl1, k16, [k2tog] twice, k2, [k2tog] twice, k20, [k2tog] twice, k1.
Cast off. With rs facing, rejoin yarn to rem 78 sts.
Shape right leg
Next row k to end.
Work 45 rows in st st. Cont in st st, but dec 1 st at each end on next row and every foll alt row until 34 sts. Work 6 rows in st st. Change to 3 mm (no. 11/US 2–3) needles.
Row 1 sl1, k1, * p1, k1 *, rep from * to * to last 2 sts, k2tog.
Rows 2, 4 and 6 sl1, ** p1, k1 **, rep from ** to ** to end.
Rows 3 and 5 sl1, k1, *** p1, k1 ***, rep from *** to *** to last st, k1.
Next row sl1, k1, **** p1, k1 ****, rep from **** to **** last 3 sts, p1, inc in next st, k1.
Change to 3.25 mm (no. 10/US 3) needles.
K 2 rows.
Next row sl1, k15, turn.
Next row sl1, k9, turn.
Shape instep by working on these 10 sts only.
K 21 rows. Break off yarn. With ws facing, rejoin yarn to rem 18 sts.
Next row k18, turn.
Next row sl1, k17, pick up and k15 sts evenly along instep, k10, pick up 15 sts along other side of instep, k6.
Work 9 rows in gt st.
Shape foot
Row 1 sl1, k2, [k2tog] twice, k24, [k2tog] twice, k6, [k2tog] twice, k19.
Rows 2, 4 and 6 k to end.
Row 3 sl1, k1, [k2tog] twice, k22, [k2tog] twice, k4, [k2tog] twice, k18.
Row 5 sl1, [k2tog] twice, k20, [k2tog] twice, k2, [k2tog] twice, k17.
Cast off.

Making Up
Wash and dry all garment pieces before making up, following instructions given on ball band, to allow garment to shrink. Press all pieces (omitting ribbing) on ws using a warm iron over a damp cloth. Sew centre front seam. Sew leg seams. Beg at centre of toe, sew foot seam. Add length of twisted cord (see page 67) or ribbon to waist.

Denim mitts

See picture on page 11

Size To fit age 0–9 months
Yarn 1 x 50 g ball of 4-Ply Denim Cotton in light or dark denim (available by mail order from Little Badger) or 1 x 50 g ball of Rowan 4-Ply Cotton
Needles 1 pair of 2.75 mm (no. 12/US 2)
Tension 35 sts and 50 rows to 10 cm square over st st on 2.75 mm (no. 12/ US 2) needles after washing. Always work a tension swatch and change needles accordingly if necessary (see Basic Information, page 54).
Ability 1
Abbreviations See Basic Information, pages 54–6.
Note Denim yarn shrinks approximately 20% after washing so this garment may seem a little long when knitting. Always dec or inc using fully-fashioned method (i.e. on 3rd st from row edge).

Mitts
With 2.75 mm (no. 12/US 2) needles, loosely cast on 40 sts. Work 13 rows in k1, p1 rib.
Make ribbon holes
Next row * rib 2, m1, p2tog *, rep from * to * to end.
Next row rib to end.

Work 5 cm in ms st.
Next row k2tog, work in ms st to centre 4 sts, [k2tog] twice, work in ms st to last 2 sts, k2tog.
Rep last row 4 times.
Divide rem sts on to 2 needles and graft or cast off two sets of sts tog on wrong side.

Making Up
Wash, dry and press all garment pieces (as given for Denim coat dress, see pages 58–9). Sew seam. Use mattress stitch or neat back-stitch – do not use overstitch. Add length of twisted cord (see page 67) or ribbon to wrists.

Denim booties

See picture on page 11

Size To fit age 0–9 months
Yarn 1 x 50 g ball of 4-Ply Denim Cotton in light or dark denim (available by mail order from Little Badger) or 1 x 50 g ball of Rowan 4-Ply Cotton
Needles 1 pair of 3.25 mm (no. 10/US 3)
Tension 35 sts and 50 rows to 10 cm square over st st on 3.25 mm (no. 10/ US 3) needles after washing. Always work a tension swatch and change needles accordingly if necessary (see Basic Information, page 54).
Ability 3
Abbreviations See Basic Information, pages 54–6.
Note Denim yarn shrinks approximately 20% after washing so this garment may seem a little long when knitting. Always dec or inc using fully-fashioned method (i.e. on 3rd st from row edge).

Sole
With 3.25 mm (no. 10/US 3) needles, cast on 23 sts. K 1 row. Cont in gt st, but inc 1 st at beg on next 6 rows. K 12 rows. Cont in gt st, but dec 1 st at beg of next 6 rows. Cast off.

Upper
With 3.25 mm (no. 10/US 3) needles, cast on 65 sts. K 2 rows. Work 8 rows in k1, p1 rib. Cont in k1, p1 rib, but cast off 24 sts at beg of next rows.

Next row k5, [k2tog] 4 times, k4.
Work 11 rows in k1, p1 rib on rem 13 sts.
K 3 rows. Cast off.

Strap
With 3.25 mm (no. 10/US 3) needles, cast on 37 sts. K 1 row.
Next row k2, cast off 2 sts, k to end.
Next row k to last 4 sts, cast on 2 sts over those cast off in previous row, k to end.

Cast off.

Making Up
Wash, dry and press all garment pieces (as given for Denim coat dress, see pages 58–9). Sew back seam of Upper. Sew Upper to Sole. Sew front extension to side of Upper. Sew Strap to back of Upper, 1 cm either side of back seam. Sew button onto Upper to match buttonhole on Strap.

Quaker ridge cardigan

See picture on page 13

Size To fit age 0–6 months; 6–12 months; 1–2 years
Yarn 1 (1; 2) x 50 g ball(s) of 4-Ply Denim Cotton in dark denim (available by mail order from Little Badger) or 1 (1; 2) x 50 g ball(s) of Jaeger Siena (MC) and 2 (2; 3) x 50 g balls of 4-Ply Denim Cotton in light denim (available by mail order from Little Badger) or 2 (2; 3) x 50 g balls of Jaeger Siena (A).

Needles 1 pair each of 2.75 mm (no. 12/US 2) and 3.25 mm (no. 10/US 3)
Tension 25 sts and 35 rows to 10 cm square over st st on 3.25 mm (no. 10/US3) needles after washing. Always work a tension swatch and change needles accordingly if necessary (see Basic Information, page 54).
Ability 2
Abbreviations See Basic Information on pages 54–6.
Note Back, Left Front and Right Front are all knitted as one piece to

armhole shaping. **Denim yarn shrinks approximately 20% after washing so this garment may seem a little long when knitting.**

Always dec or inc using fully-fashioned method (i.e. on 3rd stitch from row edge).

Back, Left Front and Right Front

With MC and 2.75 mm (no. 12/US 2) needles, cast on 119 (139; 163) sts. Work 12 rows in p1, k1 rib. Change to yarn A and 3.25 mm (no. 10/US 3) needles. Work 4 rows in st st. Change to MC. K 2 rows. Rep last 6 rows a further 7 (9; 12) times if using denim cotton and 6 (8; 11) times if using plain cotton.

Divide for armholes and fronts

Next row With yarn A, k2, k2tog, k19 (24; 30), cast off 10 sts, k53 (63; 75), cast off 10 sts, k19 (24; 30), sl1, sl1 knitwise then put back onto left needle, k2tog tbl, k2.

Shape Left Front

Cont working in patt on first 22 (27; 33) sts to form Left Front, but dec 1 st on neck edge on every 4th row until 13 (17; 22) sts rem. Work a further 6 (6; 12) rows in patt ending with a MC row. Place rem 13 (17; 22) sts on stitch holder.

Shape Right Front

Work as for Left Front but rev all patterning and shaping.

Shape Back

Pick up centre 53 (63; 75) sts for Back. Work

40 (46; 46) rows, ending with yarn A. Place rem 53 (63; 75) sts on stitch holder. Cast off rem sts of Left Front to corresponding sts on Back to form left shoulder seam. Rep with Right Front and Back to form right shoulder seam, leaving 27 (29; 31) sts across Back to form neckband.

Sleeves

With MC and 2.75 mm (no. 12/US 2) needles, cast on 33 (37; 39) sts. Work 11 rows in p1, k1 rib.

Next row rib 2 (6; 8) sts, inc in next st, * rib 5, inc in next st *, rep from * to * to end of row. 38 (43; 44) sts.

Change to yarn A and 3.25 mm (no. 10/US 3) needles. Work in patt but inc 1 st at each end on 3rd row and then every foll 6th row until 55 (65; 70) sts. If using denim cotton, work a further 6 rows in patt, ending with a MC row. Cast off. Wash, dry and press all garment pieces (as given for Denim coat dress, see pages 58–9). Sew Sleeves into armhole space, sewing cast-off edge from Sleeve to vertical edge of armhole.

Sew top of sleeve seam to 10 cast-off sts from body.

Front Band

With MC and 2.75 mm (no. 12/US 2) needles, beg at bottom of Left Front and pick up 1 st for every row for first 6 rows, then pick up 2 sts for every 3 rows until beg of v-neck shaping. Then pick up 3 sts for every 4 rows around neck. Pick up 2 sts for every 3 rows up vertical right front. Work 5 rows in k1, p1 rib.

Make buttonholes

Next row work 6 sts, * cast off next 2 sts, work 10 (12; 11) sts in rib *, rep from * to * a further 3 (3; 4) times, work in rib to end.

Next row work in rib to cast off sts, ** cast on 2 sts over those cast off in previous row, work 10 (12; 11) sts in rib **, rep from ** to ** a further 2 (2; 3) times, cast on 2 sts over those cast off in previous row, work in rib to end.

Work a further 6 rows in k1, p1 rib. Cast off evenly in rib.

Cot blanket

See picture on page 15

<u>Size</u> One size (approximately 82 cm x 71 cm)

<u>Yarn</u> 3 x 50 g balls of Rowan Handknit **DK Cotton** in ecru (MC) and 1 x 50 g ball each of Rowan Handknit **DK Cotton** in pink (A), red (B), yellow (C), gold (D), light blue (E) and dark blue (F)

<u>Needles</u> 1 pair of 4 mm (no. 8/US 6)

<u>Tension</u> 20 sts and 28 rows to 10 cm square over st st on 4 mm (no. 8/US 6) needles. Always work a tension swatch and change

needles accordingly if necessary (see Basic Information, page 54).

<u>Ability</u> 4

<u>Abbreviations</u> See Basic Information, pages 54–6.

<u>Note</u> Read chart from right to left on right side rows and from left to right on wrong side rows. Work patchwork design with yarns A, B, C, D, E and F using intarsia method – do not pass yarn across back of work as this distorts image. Use separate lengths of contrast yarn for coloured area and twist yarns together on wrong side when changing colour to avoid holes.

Blanket

With MC and 4 mm (no. 8/US 6) needles, cast on 150 sts.

Next row work across 1st row of chart in MC, working in ms st where indicated.

Next row work across 2nd row of chart in MC, working in ms st where indicated.

Cont as set, working in st st or ms st and changing yarn where indicated, until chart has been completed. Cast off.

Making Up

Embroider hearts in chain st where indicated on chart. Embroider name and/or date of birth of child on top or bottom of blanket.

Chain stitch draw yarn needle up and insert again where it just came out, taking a short stitch. With needle above yarn, hold yarn with your thumb and draw it through. Rep this action to form a line of chains.

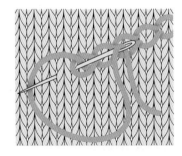

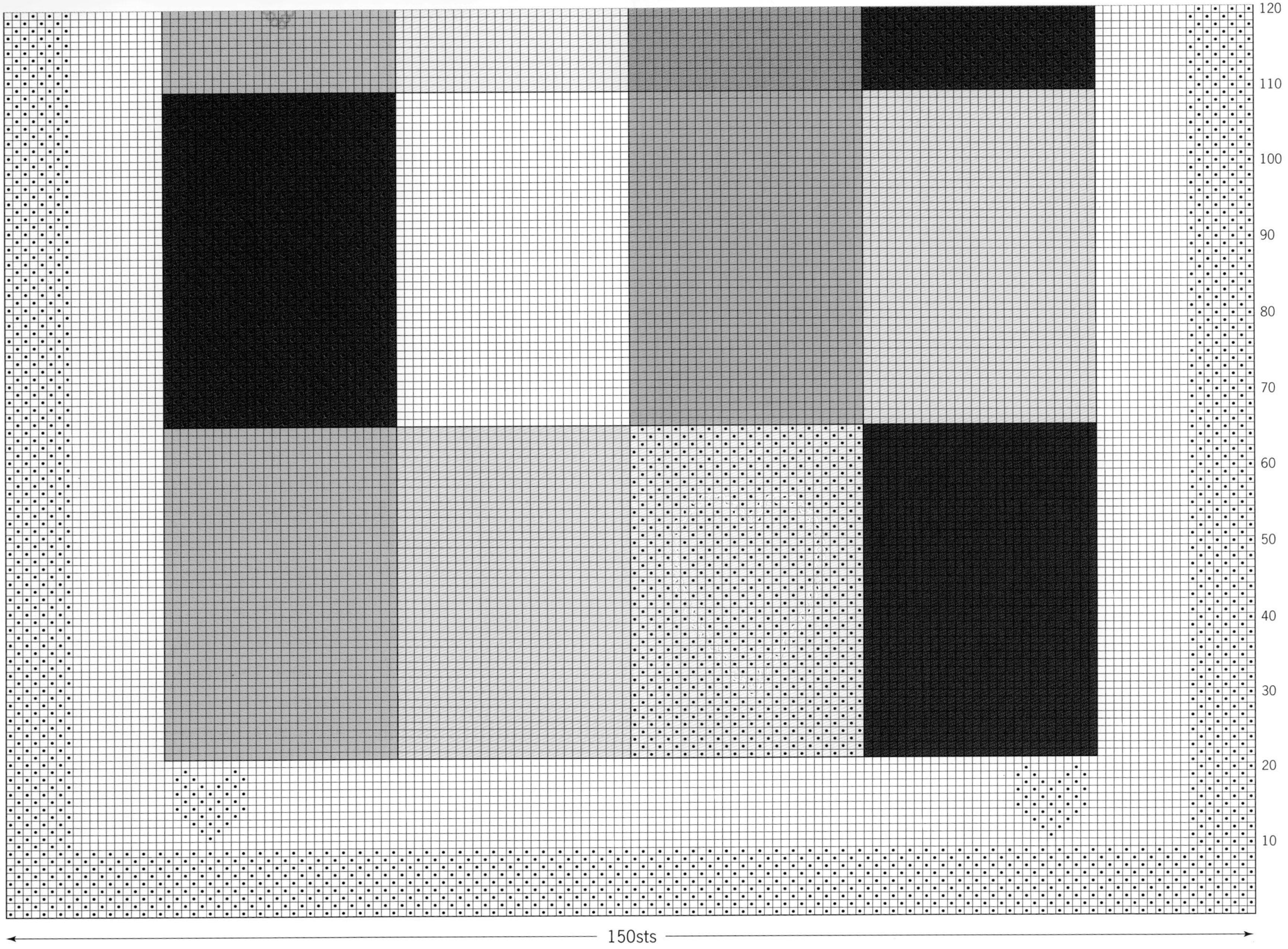

150sts

120 110 100 90 80 70 60 50 40 30 20 10

Key

| | k on rs row, p on ws row | | ecru (MC) | | red (B) | | gold (D) | | dark blue (F) |
| • | p on rs row, k on ws row | | pink (A) | | yellow (C) | | light blue (E) | ∞ | chain stitch |

Ballet cardigan

See picture on page 17

<u>Size</u> To fit age 1–3 years; 3–5 years
<u>Yarn</u> 3 (3) x 50 g balls of Rowan **DK Soft**
<u>Needles</u> 1 pair of 3.75 mm (no. 9/US 5)
<u>Tension</u> 22 sts and 31 rows to 10 cm square over st st
on 3.75 mm

(no. 9/US 5) needles. Always work a tension swatch
and change needles accordingly if necessary (see
Basic Information, page 54).
<u>Ability</u> 2
<u>Abbreviations</u> See Basic Information, pages 54–6.
<u>Note</u> Always dec or inc using fully-fashioned
method (i.e. on 3rd st from row edge).

Back

With 3.75 mm (no. 9/US 5) needles, cast on
68 (76) sts. Work 10 rows in k1, p1 rib. Cont in
st st until Back measures 17 (21) cm from
cast-on edge.

Shape raglan sleeves

Cast off 5 (7) sts at beg of next 2 rows. Cont in
st st, but dec 1 st at each end on every foll alt
row until 30 sts. Dec 1 st at each end on every
foll 4th row until 26 (28) sts. Cast off.

Left Front

With 3.75 mm (no. 9/US 5) needles, cast on
8 sts. Work 58 cm in k1, p1 rib. Cast on a
further 60 (68) sts. Work 2 rows in k1, p1 rib.
Next row work in rib to last 9 sts, k2tog, work
in rib to end.
Next row work in rib to end.
Rep last 2 rows a further 4 times. Cont in st st,
but keeping ribbed band as set and dec 1 st on
every alt row on ribbed edge, until Left Front
measures 17 (21) cm, ending with a ws row.

Shape raglan sleeve

Next row cast off 5 (7) sts, k to last 9 sts,
k2tog, work in rib to end.
Next row work 7 sts in rib, p to end.
Cont in st st, but dec 1 st at each end on next
row and every foll 3rd row a further 10 times.

Shape neck

Cont dec 1 st at beg of every 3rd row to shape
raglan sleeve, but now also dec 1 st at end on
every 4th row to shape front neck until 10 sts.
Next row k3tog, work in rib to end.
Keep rem sts on stitch holder for neckband if
grafting or cast off.

Right Front

With 3.75 mm (no. 9/US 5) needles, cast on
8 sts. Work 58 cm in k1, p1 rib. Cast on a
further 60 (68) sts. Work 2 rows in k1, p1 rib.
Next row work 7 sts in rib, sl1, k1, psso, work
in rib to end.
Next row work in rib to end.
Rep last 2 rows a further 4 times. Cont in
st st, but keeping ribbed band as set and dec
1 st on every alt row on ribbed edge until
Right Front measures 17 (21) cm ending with
a ws row.

Complete to match Left Front but rev all shaping.

Sleeves

With 3.75 mm (no. 9/US 5) needles, cast on
38 (44) sts. Work 10 rows in k1, p1 rib. Cont in
st st, but inc 1 st at each end on next row and
every foll 5th row until 56 (60) sts. Cont until
Sleeve measures 25 (30) cm from cast-on
edge, ending with a ws row.

Shape raglan sleeve

Cast off 5 (7) sts at beg on next 2 rows. Cont
in st st, but dec 1 st at each end on every foll
alt row until 4 sts. Cast off.

Making Up

Sew in sleeves. Sew side seams.

Neckband

If grafting neckband, pick up 8 sts from top of
Right Front reserved on stitch holder for
neckband, cont in k1, p1 rib until neckband
stretches across back neck, then graft 8 sts
from Left Front reserved on stitch holder for
neckband. Alternatively sew together neatly
cast off sts from Left Front and neckband.

Square-neck cardigan

See picture on page 19

<u>Size</u> To fit age 6–12 months; 1–2 years
<u>Yarn</u> 3 x 50 g balls of Jaeger Siena
<u>Needles</u> 1 pair each of 2.75 mm (no. 12/US 2) and 3 mm (no. 11/US 2–3)
<u>Tension</u> 28 sts and 38 rows to 10 cm square over st st on 3 mm (no. 11/US 2–3) needles. Always work a tension swatch and change needles accordingly if necessary (see Basic Information, page 54).
<u>Ability</u> 2
<u>Abbreviations</u> See Basic Information, pages 54–6.
<u>Note</u> Always dec or inc using fully-fashioned method (i.e. on 3rd stitch from row edge).

Back

With 2.75 mm (no. 12/US 2) needles, cast on 78 (90) sts. Work 20 rows in ms st. Change to 3 mm (no. 11/US 2–3) needles. Beg with a k row, work 65 (85) rows in st st.
Next row p15 (21), work 48 (48) sts in ms st, p to end.
Next row k15 (21), work 48 (48) sts in ms st, k to end.
Rep last 2 rows a further 15 times.

Shape neck

Next row p15 (21), work 15 (15) sts in ms st, cast off next 18 (18) sts, work 15 (15) sts in ms st, p to end.
Working on first 30 (36) sts only, dec 1 st at neck edge on next 2 rows. Place rem 28 (34) sts on stitch holder if grafting shoulder seams or cast off. With rs facing, rejoin yarn to rem 30 (36) sts and rep neck shaping for opposite side to match.

Left Front

With 2.75 mm (no. 12/US 2) needles, cast on 44 (50) sts. Work 20 rows in ms st. Change to 3 mm (no. 11/US 2–3) needles.
Next row k34 (40), work 10 sts in ms st.

Next row work 10 sts in ms st, p to end.
Rep last 2 rows a further 31 (41) times.
Next row k34 (40), work 10 sts in ms st.
Next row work 29 sts in ms st, p to end.
Next row k15 (21), work 29 sts in ms st.
Rep last 2 rows a further 9 times.

Shape neck

Next row cast off 14 sts, work 15 sts in ms st, p to end.
Next row k15 (21), work 15 sts in ms st.
Next row work 15 sts in ms st, p to end.
Rep last 2 rows.
Rows 1 and 3 k15 (21), work in ms st to last 3 sts, k2tog, work last st in ms st.
Rows 2, 4, 6 and 8 work 14 sts in ms st, p to end.
Rows 5 and 7 k15 (21), work in ms st to end.
Rep last 2 rows a further 2 (2) times. Place rem 28 (34) sts on stitch holder if grafting shoulder seams or cast off.

Right Front

Work as for Left Front but rev all patterning and shaping until 55th (75th) row has been worked.
Make buttonhole
Next row p34 (40) sts, work 4 sts in ms st, cast off 2 sts, work in ms st to end.
Next row work 4 sts in ms st, cast on 2 sts over those cast off in previous row, work 4 sts in ms st, k to end.
Complete to match Left Front, making 3 more buttonholes at intervals of 14 (14) rows.

Sleeves

With 2.75 mm (no. 12/US 2) needles, cast on 40 (44) sts. Work 18 rows in ms st. Change to 3 mm (no. 11/US 2–3). Cont in st st, but inc 1 st at each end on next row then every foll 4th row until 66 (72) sts. Work 2 (5) cm in st st, ending with a p row. Cast off.

Making Up

Graft or sew together shoulder seams. Sew in sleeves, joining cast-off edges of sleeves to vertical edges of body. Sew sleeves to 14 (16) cm below shoulder seams. Sew side seams of body. Only sew side seams to just above ms stitch hem leaving a side split. Sew sleeve seams. Use mattress stitch or neat backstitch – do not use overstitch. Sew buttons onto Left Front to match buttonholes on Right Front.

Museum sweater

See picture on page 21

<u>Size</u> To fit age 1–2 years; 2–4 years; 4–6 years.
<u>Yarn</u> 3 (3; 5) x 50 g balls of Rowan Denim
<u>Needles</u> 1 pair each of 3.25 mm (no. 10/US 3) and
4 mm (no. 8/US 6), and a 3.25 mm (no. 10/US 3)
circular needle.
<u>Tension</u> 20 sts and 28 rows to 10 cm square over st st
on 4 mm (no. 8/US 6) needles after washing. Always
work a tension swatch and change needles
accordingly if necessary (see Basic Information,
page 54).
<u>Ability</u> 2
<u>Abbreviations</u> See Basic Information, pages 54–6.
<u>Note</u> Denim yarn shrinks approximately 20% after
washing so this garment may seem a little long
when knitting. Always dec or inc using fully-
fashioned method (i.e. on 3rd stitch from row edge).

Back

With 3.25 mm (no. 10/US 3) needles, cast on
61 (67; 75) sts. Work 2.5 cm in gt st. Change to
4 mm (no. 8/US 6) needles. Cont in st st until
Back measures 22.5 (26.5; 28) cm from cast-on
edge, ending with a p row. Work patt as folls:
Next row * k1, p1 *, rep from * to * to end.
Next row p to end.
Rep last 2 rows until Back measures 42
(45.5; 50) cm from cast-on edge, ending with
a p row.

Shape shoulders

Cast off 21 (22; 25) sts at each end on next
row. Place rem 19 (23; 25) sts across centre
on stitch holder for neckband.

Front

Work as for Back until Front measures 28
(31.5; 34) cm from cast-on edge, ending with
a ws row.

Shape panels

Work 28 (31; 35) sts in patt as set, turn.
Work on this set of sts only. Cont working in
patt as set until Front measures 34 (38; 42) cm
from cast-on edge, ending with a ws row.

Shape neck

Dec 1 st at neck edge on next 3 (4; 4) rows and
every foll 4 (5; 6) alt rows. Cont working on
rem 21 sts until Front measures 42 (45.5; 50)
cm from cast-on edge. Cast off. With rs
facing, slip centre 5 sts on stitch holder for
buttonhole band and button band, rejoin yarn
to rem 28 (31; 35) sts and rep shaping for
opposite side to match.

Sleeves

With 3.25 mm (no. 10/US 3) needles, cast on
24 (30; 36) sts. Work 2.5 (2.5; 2.5) cm in gt st.
Change to 4 mm (no. 8/US 3) needles. Cont in
st st, but inc 1 st at each end of next row and
every foll 5th row until 44 (56; 62) sts. Cont in
st st until Sleeve measures 25.5 (31.5; 37) cm
from cast-on edge. Cast off.

Neckband

Wash and dry all garment pieces before
making up, following instructions given on
ball band, to allow garment to shrink. Press
all pieces (omitting ribbing) on ws using a
warm iron over a damp cloth. Sew shoulder
seams with neat backstitch. With a 3.25 mm
(no. 10/US 3) circular needle, pick up sts
around neck. Pick up all 19 (23; 25) sts from
Back reserved on stitch holder for neckband,
but miss every 4th st on either side of Front
neck edge. Work 2.5 cm in gt st. Cast off.

Buttonhole Band

With 3.25 mm (no. 10/US 3) needles, pick up
5 sts reserved on stitch holder for buttonhole
and button band. Work 1.5 (1.5; 2.5) cm in gt st.
Make buttonhole
Next row k1, k2tog, k2.
Next row k2, m1, k2.
Work 3.5 (3.5; 2.5) cm in gt st. Make a second
buttonhole using method given above. Work
3.5 cm in gt st. Make a third buttonhole using
the method given above. Work 2 rows in gt st.
Cast off.

Button Band

Rejoin yarn to back of 5 sts reserved on stitch
holder for buttonhole and button band. Cont
in gt st until button band measures to top of
neckband when slightly stretched. Cast off.

Making Up

Sew buttonhole band and button band neatly to
body, taking particular care at bottom corners.
Sew in sleeves, joining cast-off edge to vertical
edge of body. Sew sleeves to 12.5 (14; 16) cm
below shoulder seams. Sew sleeve seams. Sew
side seams of body. Use mattress stitch or neat
backstitch – do not use overstitch. Sew buttons
on to button band to match buttonholes.

Quaker ridge pixie hat

See picture on page 23

Size To fit age 1–2 years; 2–4 years; 4–6 years

Yarn 1 (1; 1) x 50 g ball of 4-Ply Denim Cotton in dark denim (MC) and 1 (1; 1) x 50 g ball of 4-Ply Denim Cotton in light denim (A) (both available by mail order from Little Badger)

Needles 1 pair each of 2.75 mm (no. 12/US 2) and 3.25 mm (no. 10/US 3)

Tension 35 sts and 50 rows to 10 cm square over st st on 3.25 mm (no. 10/US 3) needles after washing. Always work a tension swatch and change needles accordingly if necessary (see Basic Information, page 54).

Ability 2

Abbreviations See Basic Information, pages 54–6.

Note Always dec or inc using fully-fashioned method (i.e. on 3rd stitch from row edge).

Hat

With MC and 2.75 mm (no. 12/US 2) needles, cast on 100 (109; 121) sts. Work 25 (27; 27) rows in k1, p1 rib. Change to yarn A and 3.25 mm (no. 10/US 3) needles. Work 4 rows in st st. Change to MC. K 2 rows (this forms the ridge). Rep last 6 rows a further 2 (3; 4) times. Change to yarn A. Work 4 rows in st st. Change to MC.

Shape crown

Next row * k7 (7; 8), k2tog *, rep from * to * to last st, k1.

Next row k to end.

Change to yarn A. Work 4 rows in st st. Change to MC.

Next row ** k6 (6; 7), k2tog **, rep from ** to ** to last st, k1.

Next row k to end.

Cont dec as set until k1, k2tog has been worked.

Next row k to end.

Change to yarn A. Work 4 rows in st st. Change to MC.

Next row *** k2tog ***, rep from *** to *** to last st, k1.

Next row k to end.

Change to yarn A. Work 4 rows in st st. Change to MC.

Next row **** k2tog ****, rep from **** to **** to last st, k1.

Making Up

Thread yarn end twice through rem sts and pull up tight. Leave a 30 cm length of yarn for attaching tassle if not using twisted cord. Wash and dry all garment pieces before making up, following instructions given on ball band, to allow garment to shrink. Press all pieces (omitting ribbing) on ws using a warm iron over a damp cloth. Sew seam with mattress stitch or neat backstitch – do not use overstitch. Use a length of twisted cord or 30 cm of yarn to attach tassle to hat.

Twisted Cord

A twisted cord is made by twisting strands of yarn together. The thickness of the cord depends on the number and weight of strands.

Cut strands four times desired finished length and allow a little extra for knotting. Knot strands about 2.5 cm from each end. Place one end over door knob and put a pencil through other end. Turn pencil clockwise until strand are tightly twisted. Keeping strands taut, fold piece in half. Take cord from doorknob, remove pencil and allow cord to twist onto itself. Make sure each end if knotted securely.

Tassle

Wrap yarn around a piece of cardboard that is the length required for the tassle, leaving a 30 cm strand loose at either end. With a yarn needle, knot both sides to the first loop and run the loose strand under the wrapped strands. Pull tightly and tie at the top. Cut the lower edge of the tassle and, holding the tassle about 2 cm from the top, wind the top strands (one clockwise and one counter-clockwise) around the tassle. Thread the two strands and insert them through to the top of the tassle.

Crossover-back sweater

See picture on page 25

Size To fit age 6–12 months
Yarn 4 x 50 g balls of Jaeger Siena
Needles 1 pair each of 3 mm (no. 11/US 2-3) and 2.75 mm (no. 12/US 2)
Tension 28 sts and 38 rows to 10 cm square over st st on 3 mm (no. 11/US 2-3) needles. Always work a tension swatch and change needles accordingly if necessary (see Basic Information, page 54).

Ability 3
Abbreviations See Basic Information, pages 54–6.
Note Read chart from right to left on right side rows and from left to right on wrong side rows. Always dec or inc using fully-fashioned method (i.e. on 3rd stitch from row edge).

Front

With 2.75 mm (no. 12/US 2) needles, cast on 72 sts. K 8 rows. Change to 3 mm (no. 11/US 2-3) needles. Beg with a k row, work 37 rows in st st.
Next row p26, work across 1st row of chart in ms st where indicated, p25.
Next row k25, work across 2nd row of chart in ms st where indicated, k26.
Cont as set until chart is completed. Work 20 rows in st st. Work 7 rows in ms st.
Shape neck
Next row work 30 sts in ms st, turn.
Work on this set of sts only. Dec 1 st at neck edge on next 7 rows, on foll 2 alt rows and then on foll 3rd row until 20 sts. Work 3 rows in ms st. Keep rem 20 sts on stitch holder if grafting shoulder seams or cast off. With rs facing, place centre 12 sts on stitch holder for neckband, rejoin yarn to rem 30 sts and work in ms st to end. Rep neck shaping for opposite side to match.

Left Back

With 2.75 mm (no. 12/US 2) needles, cast on 52 sts. K 8 rows. Change to 3 mm (no. 11/US 2–3) needles.

Next row k to end.
Next row p to last 5 sts, k to end.
Rep last 2 rows a further 42 times.
Next row k to end.
Next row * p1, k1 *, rep from * to * to last 5 sts, k to end.
Next row k5, ** p1, k1**, rep from ** to ** to last 1 st, p1.
Rep last 2 rows a further 11 times.
Next row *** p1, k1 ***, rep from *** to *** to last 5 sts, k to end.
Place first 32 sts on stitch holder for neckband. Graft rem 20 sts to those reserved on stitch holder from Front to form left shoulder.

Right Back

Work as for Left Back but rev all patterning and shaping.

Sleeves

With 2.75 mm (no. 12/US 2) needles, cast on 34 sts. K 8 rows. Change to 3 mm (no. 11/US 2–3) needles. Working centre 34 sts in ms st and all other sts in st st, inc 1 st at each end on next row and every foll fourth row until 66 sts. Cont as set, work in ms st and st st for 2 cm. Cast off.

Neckband

With 2.75 mm (no. 12/US 2) needles, pick up sts around neck. Pick up all 32 sts from Left and Right Backs and all 12 sts from Front reserved on stitch holders for neckband, but miss every 4th st on either side of Front neck edge. Work 0.5 cm in gt st. Make an eyelet buttonhole at each end of the next row 0.5 cm in from either edge. To make an eyelet buttonhole, work to buttonhole, k2tog, yon, cont to end of row, then on return row, work the yon as a stitch. Work a further 0.5 cm in gt st. Cast off.

Making Up

Sew in sleeves, joining cast-off edges of sleeves to vertical edges of body and placing centre of sleeves to shoulder seams. Take care to match ms st panels of sleeves to those of body. Sew sleeves to 13cm below shoulder seams. Sew side seams of body. Sew sleeve seams. Use mattress stitch or a neat backstitch – do not use overstitch. Sew buttons onto Left and Right Backs to match buttonholes.

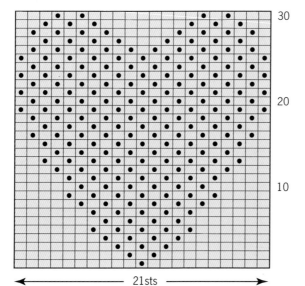

30

20

10

21sts

Key

⬜ k on rs row, p on ws row

◉ p on rs row, k on ws row

Dragon hat

See picture on page 27

Size To fit age 2–4 years

Yarn 2 x 50 g balls of Rowan Handknit **DK** Cotton in green (MC) and
1 x 50 g ball each of Rowan Handknit **DK** Cotton in orange (A) and
black (B).

Needles 1 pair of 3.25 mm (no. 10/US 3) and 2 pairs of 4 mm (no. 8/US 6)

Tension 20 sts and 28 rows to 10 cm square over st st on 4 mm (no. 8/US 6) needles. Always work a tension swatch and change needles accordingly if necessary (see Basic Information, page 54).

Ability 5

Abbreviations See Basic Information, pages 54–6.

Note Always dec or inc using fully-fashioned method (i.e. on 3rd st from row edge).

Hat

With MC and 3.25mm (no. 10/US 3) needles, cast on 91 sts. K 8 rows. Change to 4 mm (no. 8/US 6) needles.

Shape nostrils

Row 1 k40. Change to 3.25 mm (no. 10/US 3) needles and yarn A. Cast on 18 sts, k next 11 sts from main piece of work with yarn A, cast on 18 sts with yarn A, turn. Change to 4 mm (no. 8/US 6) needles. Work 5 rows in st st on 47 orange sts, beg with a p row. Cast off 47 orange sts. Sew short edges of orange strip tog to make a ring. Change to MC. Cont row 1 by picking up and knitting sts from cast-on orange edge, 17 sts from before seam and 18 sts from beyond seam. (This will bring you back to rem 40 green sts.) K 40.

Row 2 p40, k35, p40.

Row 3 k40, p35, k40.

Row 4 p39, p2tog, p33, p2tog tbl, p to end.

Row 5 cast on 8 sts, k47, ssk, k13, ssk, k1, k2tog, k13, k2tog, k to end.

Row 6 cast on 8 sts, p47, p2tog, p27, p2tog tbl, p to end.

Row 7 k7, k2tog, k38, ssk, k10, ssk, k1, k2tog, k10, k2tog, k38, ssk, k7.

Rows 8, 10 and 12 p to end.

Row 9 k6, k2tog, k38, ssk, k8, ssk, k1, k2tog, k8, k2tog, k38, ssk, k6.

Rows 11 and 13 cont dec as set.

Row 14 p3, p2tog tbl, p to last 5 sts, p2tog, p3.

Row 15 k2, k2tog, k to last 4 sts, ssk, k2.

Row 16 p1, p2tog tbl, p to last 3 sts, p2tog, p1.

Row 17 k2tog, k43, [inc in next st] twice, k to last 2 sts, ssk.

Row 18 cast on 10 sts, p to end.

Row 19 cast on 10 sts, k10, ssk, [k13, ssk] twice, k12, inc in next st, k2, inc in next st, [k13, k2tog] 3 times, k10.

Row 20 p9, p2tog tbl, p to last 11 sts, p2tog, p9.

Row 21 k8, sl2tog, k1, p2sso, [k12, ssk] twice, k11, inc in next st, [k12, k2tog] twice, k12, k3tog, k4, inc in next st, k8.

Row 22 p7, p2tog tbl, p37, inc in next st, p6, inc in next st, p38, p2tog, p7.

Row 23 k6, sl2tog, k1, p2sso, [k11, ssk] twice, k10, inc in next st, [k11, k2tog] twice, k11, k3tog, k6.

Rows 24, 25 and 26 cont dec as set.

Row 27 k2, sl2tog, k1, p2sso, [k9, ssk] twice, k16, fold work back with ws facing, using third needle k 1 st from front needle, cast off all recently inc sts to form 1st fin taking 1 st from each needle, slip last st on to original rh, keep yarn on an even tension and cont row, including dec as set.

Row 28 p1, p2tog tbl, p to last 3 sts, p2tog, p1.

Row 29 sl2tog, k1, p2sso, [k8, ssk] twice, k7, inc in next st twice, [k8, k2tog] twice, k8, sl2tog, k1, p2sso.

Row 30 cast on 10 sts, p to end.

Row 31 cast on 10 sts, k10, ssk, cont shaping as set.

Row 32 p9, p2tog tbl, p to last 11 sts, p2tog, p9.

Row 33 k8, sl2tog, k1, p2sso, [k6, ssk] twice, k6, inc in next st, k6, k2tog, k6, k3tog, k8.

Row 34 p7, p2tog tbl, p19, inc in next st, p6, inc in next st, p to last 9 sts, p2tog, p7.

Row 35 k6, sl2tog, k1, p2sso, [k5, ssk] twice, k5, inc in next st, k7, inc in next st, [k5, k2tog] twice, k5, k3tog, k6.

Row 36 p5, p2tog tbl, p17, inc in next st, p9, inc in next st, p7, p2tog, p5.

Row 37 k4, sl2tog, k1, p2sso, [k4, ssk] twice, k4, inc in next st, k11, inc in next st, [k4, k2tog] twice, k3, k3tog, k2.

Row 38 p3, p2tog, p14, inc in next st, p13, inc in next st, p14, p2tog, p3.

Row 39 k2, sl2tog, k1, p2sso, [k3, ssk] twice, k3, inc in next st, k15, inc in next st, [k3, k2tog] twice, k3, k3tog, k2.

Row 40 p1, p2tog tbl, p to last 3 sts, p2tog, p1.

Row 41 sl2tog, k1, p2sso, [k2, ssk] twice, k11, fold work back with ws facing, cast off inc sts as before, [k2, k2tog] twice, sl2tog, k1, p2sso, transfer rem sts to other needle, cut off yarn leaving a long end, thread twice through rem sts and draw up into a tight circle. Sew along the back fins using mattress st.

Tail

With MC and 3.25mm (no. 10/US 3) needles, cast on 11sts. Work 15 cm in st st, ending with a k row.

Next row cast off 3 sts purlwise, p to end.

Next row cast off 3 sts, cast on 4 sts, k5, [inc in next st] twice, k2.

Next row cast on 4 sts purlwise, p to end.

Next row k6, [inc in next st] twice, k7.

Next row p to end.

Cont inc at either side of centre on k rows until 23 sts.

Next row p11.

Fold work back with ws facing, with 3rd needle k 1 st from front needle, cast off taking 1 st from each needle). Turn to rs and sew up to make an arrowhead for tail end.

Making Up

Sew tail to back of hat just below last fin. With yarn B, make 2 circular eyes approximately 1 cm in diameter by overstitching. Place eyes on either side of 1st fin at front of hat with a gap of 3 sts between them.

Pirate sweater

See picture on page 29

See picture on page 29

Size To fit age 1–2 years; 2–4 years; 4–6 years
Yarn 5 (7; 8) x 50 g balls of Rowan Handknit DK Cotton in navy (MC) and 1 x 50 g ball of Rowan Handknit DK Cotton in ecru (A)
Needles 1 pair each of 3.25 mm (no. 10/US 3) and 4 mm (no. 8/US 6)
Tension 20 sts and 28 rows to 10 cm square over st st on 4 mm (no. 8/US 6) needles. Always work a tension swatch and change needles accordingly if necessary (see Basic Information, page 54).

Ability 3
Abbreviations See Basic Information, pages 54–6.
Note Read chart from right to left on right side rows and from left to right on wrong side rows. Work skull and crossbones design with yarn A using intarsia method – do not pass yarn across back of work as this distorts image. Use separate lengths of contrast yarn for coloured area and twist yarns together on the wrong side when changing colour to avoid holes. Always dec or inc using fully-fashioned method (i.e. on 3rd stitch from row edge).

Back
With yarn A and 3.25 mm (no. 10/US 3) needles, cast on 65 (73; 81) sts. Change to MC. K 16 rows. Change to 4 mm (no. 8/US 6) needles. Beg with a k row, work 54 (65; 71) rows in st st.
Shape armholes
Cast off 4 (5; 5) sts at beg of next 2 rows. Work 39 (38; 45) rows in st st.
Shape shoulders and shoulder fastening
For sizes 1–2 and 2–4 years
Place first 15 (18) sts on stitch holder for shoulder fastening. Place centre 27 (27) sts on stitch holder for neckband. Cast off rem 15 (18) sts to shape right shoulder. With ws facing, rejoin yarn to 15 (18) sts reserved on stitch holder for shoulder fastening. Work 6 rows in gt st. Cast off.
For size 4–6 years
Cast off 20 sts to shape right shoulder. Place centre 31 sts on stitch holder for neckband. With rs facing, rejoin yarn to rem 20 sts. Work 5 rows in gt st. Cast off.

Front
Work as given for Back until 12 (19; 19) rows of st st have been completed.
For size 1–2 years
Next row k11 with MC, k across 1st row of chart A, k12 with MC.
Next row p12 with MC, p across 2nd row of chart A, p11 with MC.
For size 2–4 and 4–6 years
Next row p17 (18) with MC, p across 1st row of chart A (B), p15 (9) with MC.
Next row k15 (9) with MC, k across 2nd row of chart A (B), p17 (18) with MC.
Cont as set until 42nd (46th; 52nd) row of chart has been worked.
Shape armholes
Cont working from chart, but cast off 4 (5; 5) sts at beg of next 2 rows. Cont as set until 60th (60th; 76th) row of chart has been completed. Work 10 (10; 7) rows in st st with MC.

Shape neck
For sizes 1–2 and 4–6 years
Next row k23 (29), turn.
Work on this set of sts only. Dec 1 st at neck edge on next 6 (6) rows, then on foll 2 (3) alt rows. Work 2 (3) rows in st st.
Make shoulder fastening
K 2 rows.
Make buttonholes
Next row k4 (5), cast off next 2 sts, k5 (6), cast off next 2 sts, k to end.
Next row k2 (3), cast on 2 sts over those cast off in previous row, k5 (6), cast on 2 sts over those cast off in previous row, k to end.
K 2 rows. Cast off rem 15 (20) sts. Place centre 11 (13) sts on stitch holder for neckband. With rs facing, rejoin yarn to rem 23 (29) sts and k to end. Rep neck shaping for opposite side to match, but cast off sts once neck shaping is complete.
For sizes 2–4 years
Next row p27, turn.
Work on this set of sts only. Dec 1 st at neck edge on next 7 rows, then on foll 2 alt rows. Cont in st st for 4 rows. Cast off rem 18 sts for right shoulder. Place centre 9 sts on stitch holder for neckband. With ws facing, rejoin yarn to rem 27 sts and p to end. Rep neck shaping for opposite side to match, but do not cast off once neck shaping is complete.
Make shoulder fastening
K 2 rows.
Make buttonholes
Next row k6, cast off next 2 sts, k7, cast off next 2 sts, k to end.
Next row k3, cast on 2 sts over those cast off in previous row, k7, cast on 2 sts over those cast off in previous row, k to end.
K 1 row. Cast off rem 18 sts.

Sleeves
With yarn A and 3.25 mm (no. 10/US 3) needles, cast on 38 (40; 40) sts. Change to MC and k 10 rows. Change to 4 mm (no. 8/US 3) needles. Cont in st st, but inc 1 st at each end on next row and every foll 8th row until 52 (56; 60) sts. Cont in st st until Sleeve measures 22 (28; 34) cm. Cast off.

Neck
Sew right shoulder seam. With MC and 3.25 mm (no. 10/US 3) needles, pick up sts around neck. Pick up all 27 (27; 31) sts from Back and all 11 (9; 13) sts from Front reserved on stitch holders for neckband, but miss every 4th st on either side of Front neck edge. K 2 rows. Cont in gt st, but make a buttonhole on left side of neck in next row on 3rd and 4th sts from edge using method described above. K 3 rows. Change to yarn A. Cast off evenly but not too tightly.

Making Up
Sew left shoulder seam. Sew in sleeves, joining cast off edges of sleeves to vertical edges of body. When sewing in sleeves, attach top 2 cm of side seams to 4 (5; 5) cast off sts on body. When sewing in left sleeve, overlap left shoulder fastening on Back with left shoulder fastening on Front. Sew side seams of body. Only sew side seams to just above gt st hem leaving a side split. Sew sleeve seams. Use mattress stitch or neat backstitch – do not use overstitch. Sew buttons on to left shoulder fastening to match buttonholes. Using MC, add cross stitches to skull and crossbones motif where indicated on chart.

Cross stitch draw yarn needle up and make a diagonal stitch to upper left corner. Bring needle back up in lower left corner and make a diagonal stitch to upper right corner.

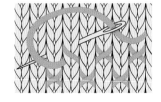

Chart A

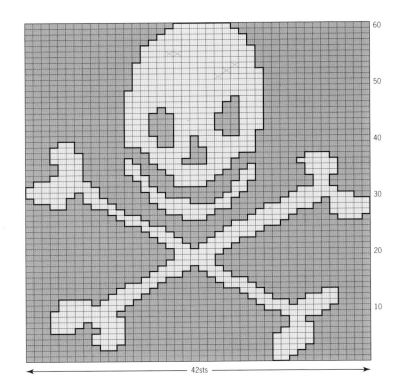

Chart B

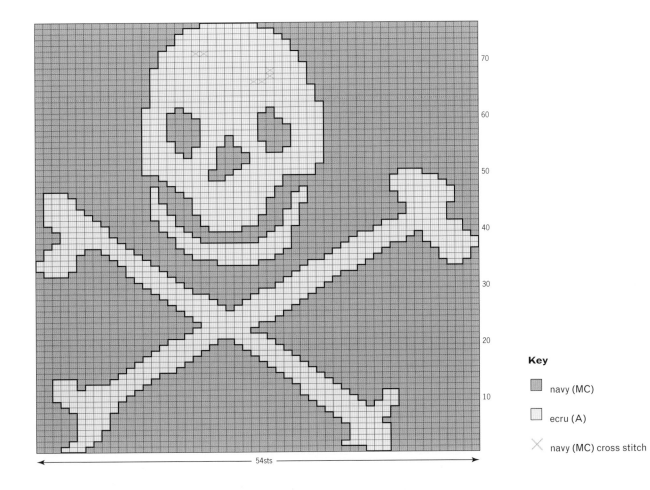

Key

▨ navy (MC)

▦ ecru (A)

✕ navy (MC) cross stitch

Sunflower sweater

See picture on page 31

<u>Size</u> To fit age 2–4 years; 4–6 years

<u>Yarn</u> 8 (9) x 50 g balls of Jaeger Pure Cotton in cream (MC) and 1 (1) x 50 g ball each of Jaeger Pure Cotton in red (A), orange (B) and yellow (C)

<u>Needles</u> 1 pair each of 3 mm (no. 11/US 2–3) and 3.25 mm (no. 10/US 3)

<u>Tension</u> 25 sts and 34 rows to 10 cm square over st st on 3.25 mm (no. 10/US 3) needles. Always work a tension swatch and change needles accordingly if necessary (see Basic Information, page 54).

<u>Ability</u> 4

<u>Abbreviations</u> See Basic Information, pages 54–6.

<u>Note</u> Read chart from right to left on right side rows and from left to right on wrong side rows. Work sunflower design with yarns A, B and C using intarsia method – do not pass yarn across back of work as this distorts image. Use separate lengths of contrast yarn for coloured area and twist yarns together on wrong side when changing colour to avoid holes. Always dec or inc using fully-fashioned method (i.e. on 3rd st from row edge).

Back

With yarn B and 3 mm (no. 11/US 2–3) needles, cast on 73 (81) sts. Beg with a k row, work 4 rows in st st. Change to yarn C. Work 3 rows in st st. Change to MC. P 1 row. Change to 3.25 mm (no. 10/US 3) needles. Work 66 (72) rows in st st.

Shape sleeves

Cast off 5 sts at beg of next 2 rows. Work 40 (44) rows in st st. Cast off first 16 (20) sts to shape right shoulder, place centre 31 sts on stitch holder for neckband.

Shape left shoulder fastening

Work 6 rows in gt st with rem 20 sts. Cast off.

Front

With yarn B and 3 mm (no. 11/US 2–3) needles, cast on 73 (81) sts. Beg with a k row, work 4 rows in st st. Change to yarn C. Work 3 rows in st st. Change to MC. P 1 row. Change to 3.25 mm (no. 10/US 3) needles. Work 14 (24) rows in st st.

Next row k 14 (18) sts with MC, k across 1st row of chart, k 15 (19) with MC.

Next row p 15 (19) with MC, p across 2nd row of chart, p 14 (18) with MC.

Cont as set until 52nd (48th) row of the chart has been worked.

Shape armholes

Cont working from chart, but cast off 5 sts at beg of next 2 rows. Cont as set until chart has been completed. Work 12 (10) rows in st st.

Shape neck

Next row k 24 (30) sts, turn.

Work on this set of sts only. Cont in st st, but

dec 1 st at neck edge on next 6 (8) rows, then on foll 2 alt rows. Work 5 rows in st st.

Make left shoulder fastening

K 2 rows.

Make buttonholes

Next row k 3, cast off next 2 sts, k 6 (7), cast off next 2 sts, k to end.

Next row k 3 (6), cast on 2 sts over those cast off in previous row, k 6 (7), cast on 2 sts over those cast off in previous row, k to end.

K 2 rows. Cast off rem 16 (20) sts. With rs facing, slip centre 15 (11) sts on stitch holder for neckband, rejoin yarn to rem 24 (30) sts and k to end. Rep neck shaping for opposite side to match, but cast off sts once neck shaping is complete.

Sleeves

With yarn A and 3 mm (no. 11/US 2–3) needles, cast on 42 (46) sts. K 8 rows. Change to yarn B and 3.25 mm (no. 12/US 3) needles. Work 4 rows in st st. Change to yarn C. Work 3 rows in st st. Change to MC. Cont in st st, but inc 1 st at each end of next row and every foll 8th row until 58 (64) sts. Cont in st st until Sleeve measures 25 (30) cm. Cast off.

Neckband

Sew right shoulder seam. With yarn B and 3 mm (no. 11/US 2–3) needles, pick up sts around neck edge. Pick up all 31 (31) sts from Back and all 15 (11) sts from Front reserved on stitch holders for neckband, but miss every 4th st on either side of Front neck edge.

K 3 rows. Cont in gt st, but make a buttonhole by casting off 3rd and 4th sts from edge. K 3 rows, but remember to cast on 2 sts over those cast off in previous row. Change to yarn A. K 1 row. Cast off evenly but not too tightly.

Making Up

Sew in sleeves, joining cast-off edge of sleeves to vertical edge of body. When sewing in sleeves, attach top 2 cm of side seams to 5 cast off sts on body. When sewing in left sleeve, overlap left shoulder fastening on Back with left shoulder fastening on Front. Sew side seams of body. Only sew side seams to just above gt st hem leaving a side split. Sew sleeve seams. Use mattress stitch or neat backstitch – do not use overstitch. Sew buttons on to left shoulder fastening to match buttonholes.

Zig-zag Edging

With yarn A and 3 mm (no. 11/US 2–3) needles, cast on 6 sts. K 1 row.

Row 1 sl 1, k 1, yo, k2tog, yo, k 2.

Row 2 k 2, yo, k 2, yo, k2tog, k 1.

Row 3 sl 1, k 1, yo, k2tog, k 2, yo, k 2.

Row 4 k 2, yo, k 4, yo, k2tog, k 1.

Row 5 sl 1, k 1, yo, k2tog, k 4, yo, k 2.

Row 6 k 2, yo, k 6, yo, k2tog, k 1.

Row 7 sl 1, k 1, yo, k2tog, k2tog, k 6, yo, k 2.

Row 8 cast off 7 sts, k 2, yo, k2tog, k 1.

Rep last 8 rows until Zig-Zag Edging is long enough to reach around hem of sweater. Sew neatly onto bottom edge of sweater using flat stitch.

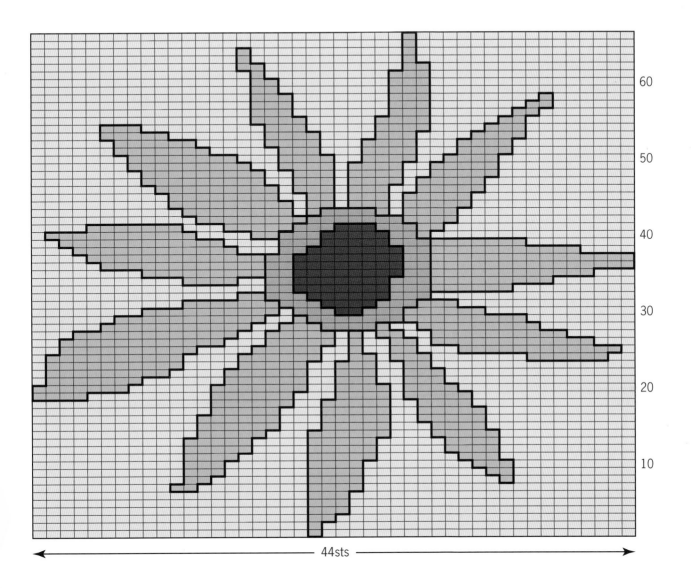

60

50

40

30

20

10

44sts

Key

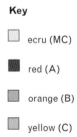

ecru (MC)

red (A)

orange (B)

yellow (C)

Starfish jacket

See picture on page 33

Size To fit age 2–4 years; 4–6 years
Yarn 8 (9) x 50 g balls of Rowan Handknit DK Cotton in plum (MC) and 1 (1) x 50 g ball each of Rowan Handknit DK Cotton in red (A), light blue (B), yellow (C) and green (D).
Needles 1 pair each of 3.25 mm (no. 10/US 3) and 4 mm (no. 8/US 6)
Tension 20 sts and 28 rows to 10 cm square over st st on 4 mm (no. 8/US 6) needles. Always work a tension swatch and change needles accordingly if necessary (see Basic Information, page 54).

Ability 5
Abbreviations See Basic Information, pages 54–6.
Note Read chart from right to left on rs rows and from left to right on ws rows. Work starfish designs with yarns A, B, C and D using intarsia method – do not pass yarn across back of work as this distorts image. Use separate lengths of contrast yarn for coloured area and twist yarns together on ws when changing colour to avoid holes. Always dec or inc using fully-fashioned method (i.e. on 3rd st from row edge).

Back

With yarn D and 3.25 mm (no. 10/US 3) needles, cast on 73 (81) sts. K 8 rows. Change to MC and 4 mm (no. 8/US 6) needles.
Next row k across 1st row of chart A (B) with MC.
Next row p across 2nd row of chart A (B) with MC.
Cont as set until 70th (76th) row of chart A (B) has been worked.

Shape armholes

Cont working from chart A (B), but cast off 5 (5) sts at beg of next 2 rows. Cont as set until chart A (B) has been completed.

Shape shoulders

Cast off 19 (20) sts at each end to shape shoulders. Place rem 25 (31) sts across centre on stitch holder for neckband.

Pocket Bags

With MC and 3.25 mm (no. 10/US 3) needles, cast on 20 sts. Work 26 rows in st st. Place 20 sts on stitch holder. Work 2 pocket bags.

Left Front

With yarn D and 3.25 mm (no. 10/US 3) needles, cast on 32 (36) sts. K 8 rows. Change to MC and 4 mm (no. 8/US 6) needles.
Next row k across 1st row of chart C (D) with MC.
Next row p across 2nd row of chart C (D) with MC.
Cont as set until 34th row of chart C (D) has been completed.

Add pocket bags

Next row Cont working from chart C (D), k 6 (10) sts, place next 20 sts on stitch holder for pocket bands, k 20 sts reserved on stitch holder for pocket bags, k to end.
Cont as set until 70th (76th) row of chart C (D) has been completed.

Shape armholes

Cont working from chart C (D), but cast off 5 (5) sts at beg of next 2 rows. Cont as set until 94th (105th) row of chart C (D) has been completed.

Shape neck

Cont working from chart C (D), but dec 3 sts at neck edge of next row, dec 1 st at neck edge of next 4 rows and dec 1 st at neck edge of foll 3 (4) alt rows. Cont until 110th row of chart C (D) has been completed. Cast off rem 17 (20) sts for shoulders.

Right Front

Work as for Left Front but foll chart E (F) and rev all shaping.

Sleeves

With yarn A and 3.25 mm (no. 10/US 3) needles, cast on 40 sts. K 8 rows. Change to MC and 4 mm (no. 8/US 3) needles.
Next row k across 1st row of chart G (H) with MC.
Next row p across 2nd row of chart G (H) with MC.
Cont as set until 9th (7th) row of chart G (H) has been completed.
Cont foll chart G (H), but inc 1 st at each end of next row and every foll 8th (7th) row until 58 (64) sts. Cont until chart 88th (93rd) row of chart G (H) has been completed. Cast off.

Making Up

Sew shoulder seams. Sew in sleeves, joining cast-off edge of sleeves to vertical edges of body. When sewing in sleeves, attach top 2 cm of side seams to 4 (5) cast off sts on body. Sew side seams of body. Sew sleeve seams. Use mattress stitch or a neat backstitch – do not use overstitch.

Pocket Bands

With yarn C and 3.25 mm (no. 10/US 3) needles, pick up 20 sts reserved on stitch holder for pocket bands. K 6 rows. Cast off. Sew pocket bags neatly to inside of jacket.

Left Front Band

With yarn D and 3.25 mm (no. 10/US 3) needles, cast on 8 sts. Work in gt st until band measures from hem to neck shaping of Left Front when slightly stretched.

Right Front Band

With yarn D and 3.25 mm (no. 10/US 3) needles, cast on 8 sts. K 8 rows.
Make buttonhole
Next row k 5, cast off next 2 sts, k to end.
Next row k 1, cast on 2 sts over those cast off in previous row, k to end.
Cont in gt st, but make a further 5 buttonholes every 4 (5) cm. Cont in gt st until band measures from hem to neck shaping of Right Front when slightly stretched. Sew button bands to jacket with mattress stitch or neat flat stitch – do not use overstitch.

Neck and Collar

With MC and 3.25 mm (no. 10/US 3) needles, cast on 6 sts. K 1 row. Cont in gt st, but inc 1 st at each end of next row and every foll alt row until 12 sts. K 1 row. Cont in gt st, but inc 1 st at beg of next row and every foll alt row until 26 sts. K 52 (62) rows. Cont in gt st, but dec 1 st at end of next row and every foll alt row until 12 sts. K 1 row. Cont in gt st, but dec 1 st at each end of next row and every foll alt row until 6 sts. K 1 row. Cast off. Pin collar into position and sew into place. Pass needle through ridge on either side of work to form a neat flat seam. Join cast-on edge and cast-off edge to front at neck edge beg halfway across button band.

Chart A

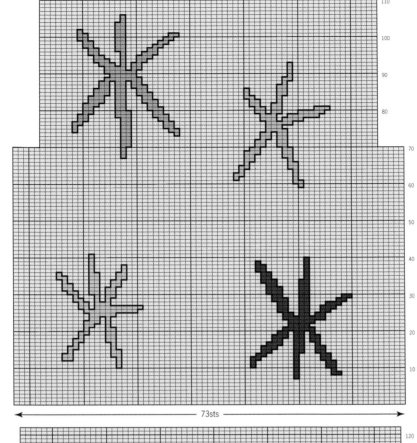

73 sts

Chart B

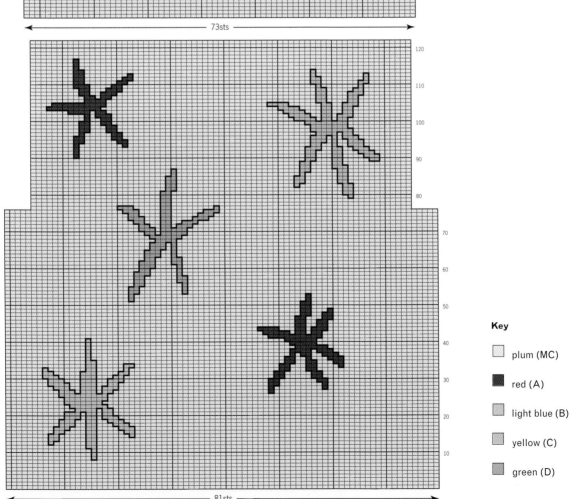

81 sts

Key

- ⬜ plum (MC)
- ⬛ red (A)
- 🟦 light blue (B)
- 🟨 yellow (C)
- 🟩 green (D)

Charts C & D

Charts E & F

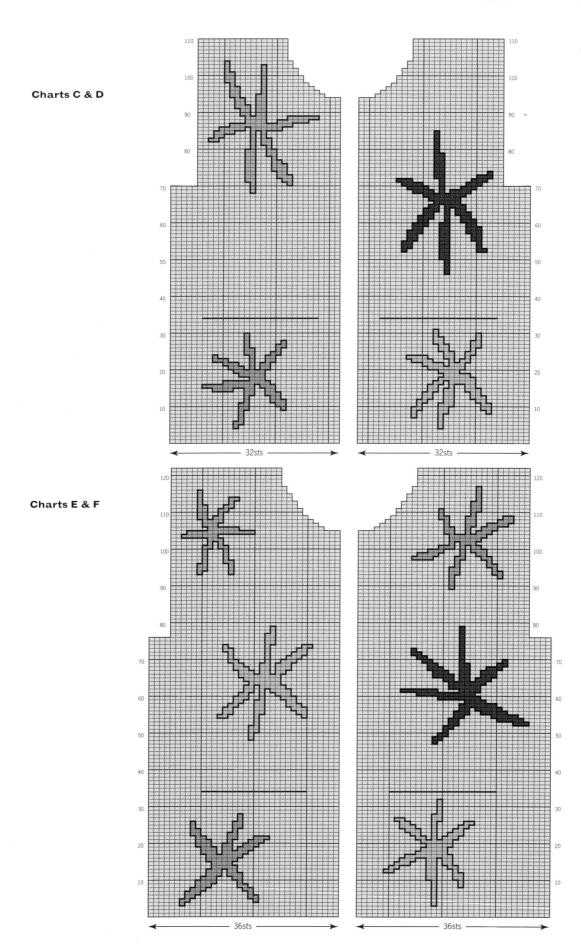

Chart G

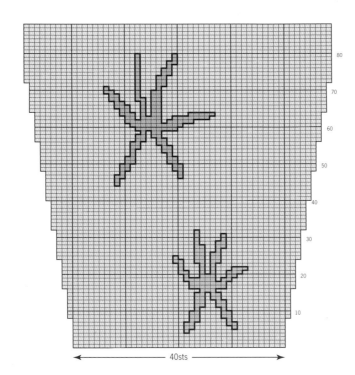

40sts

Chart H

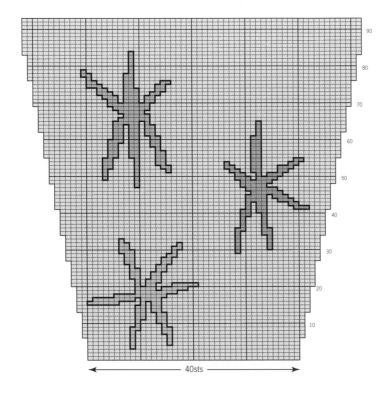

40sts

Key

☐ plum (MC)

■ red (A)

☐ light blue (B)

☐ yellow (C)

☐ green (D)

Heart sweater

See picture on page 35

<u>Size</u> To fit age 2–4 years; 4–6 years

<u>Yarn</u> 7 (8) x 50 g balls of Rowan Handknit **DK** Cotton in pink (**MC**) and 1 x 50 g ball of **D**yed in the Wool Cotton Chenille in cherry (**A**)

<u>Needles</u> 1 pair each of 3.25 mm (no. 10/US 3) and 4 mm (no. 8/US 6)

<u>Tension</u> 20 sts and 28 rows to 10 cm square over st st on 4 mm (no. 8/US 6) needles. Always work a tension swatch and change needles accordingly if necessary (see Basic Information, page 54).

<u>Ability</u> 3

<u>Abbreviations</u> See Basic Information, pages 54–6.

<u>Note</u> Read chart from right to left on right side rows and from left to right on wrong side rows. Work heart design with yarn A using intarsia method – do not pass yarn across back of work as this distorts image. Use separate lengths of contrast yarn for coloured area and twist yarns together on wrong side when changing colour to avoid holes. Always dec or inc using fully-fashioned method (i.e. on 3rd st from row edge).

Back

With MC and 3.25 mm (no. 10/US 3) needles, cast on 72 (81) sts. Work 16 rows in ms st. Change to 4 mm (no. 8/US 6) needles. Beg with a k row, work 58 (64) rows in st st.

Shape armholes

Cast off 5 sts at beg of next 2 rows. Work 34 (44) rows in st st.

Shape shoulders

Cast off 17 (20) sts at each end on next row to shape shoulders. Keep rem 28 (31) sts across centre on stitch holder for neckband.

Front

Work as for Back until 12 (20) rows of st st have been completed.

Next row k 19 (24) with MC, k across 1st row of chart, k 20 (24) with MC.

Next row p 20 (24) with MC, p across 2nd row of chart, p 19 (24) with MC.

Cont as set until 20th (25th) row of chart has been worked.

Shape armholes

Cont working from chart, but cast off 5 sts at beg on next 2 rows. Cont as set until chart has been completed. Work 17 (23) rows in st st.

Shape neck

Next row p 26 (28), turn.

Work on this set of sts only. Dec 1 st at neck edge on next 6 (5) rows, then on foll 3 alt rows. Work 3 (6) rows in st st. Cast off rem 17 (20) sts for shoulder. With the wrong side facing, slip centre 10 (15) sts on stitch holder for neckband, rejoin yarn to rem 26 (28) sts and p to end. Rep neck shaping for opposite side to match.

Sleeves

With MC and 3.25 mm (no. 10/US 3) needles, cast on 38 (40) sts. Work 12 rows in ms st. Change to 4 mm (no. 8/US 3) needles. Cont in st st, but inc 1 st at each end of next row, then every foll 6th (8th) row until 58 (60) sts. Cont in st st until Sleeve measures 26 (33) cm. Cast off.

Neckband

Sew right shoulder seam. With MC and 3.25 mm (no. 10/US 3) needles, pick up sts around neck edge. Pick up all 28 (31) sts from Back and all 10 (15) sts from Front reserved on stitch holders for neckband, but miss every 4th st on either side of Front neck edge. Work 2.5 cm in k 1, p 1 rib, then 6 rows in st st. Cast off evenly but not too tightly. The st st rows will roll to front.

Making Up

Sew left shoulder seam. Sew in sleeves, joining cast-off edges of sleeves to vertical edges of body. Sew side seams of body. Only sew side seam to just above ms st hem leaving a side split. Sew sleeve seams. Use mattress stitch or a neat backstitch – do not use overstitch.

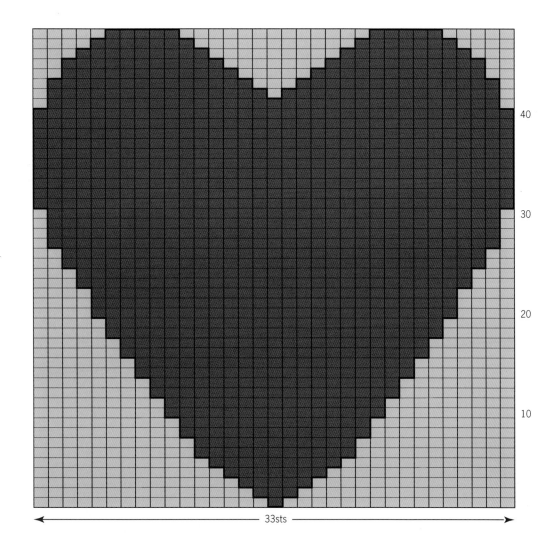

40

30

20

10

◄─────────── 33sts ───────────►

Key

pink (MC)

cherry (A)

Soccer sweater

See picture on page 37

Size To fit age 1–2 years; 2–4 years; 4–6 years
Yarn 5 (7; 8) x 50 g balls of Jaeger Pure Cotton in black (MC) and 1 x 50 g ball of Jaeger Pure Cotton in ecru (A)
Needles 1 pair each of 3 mm (no. 11/US 2) and 3.25 mm (no. 10/US 3)
Tension 25 sts and 34 rows to 10 cm square over st st on 3.25 mm (no. 10/US 3) needles. Always work a tension swatch and change needles accordingly if necessary (see Basic Information, page 54).

Ability 3
Abbreviations See Basic Information, pages 54–6.
Note Read chart from right to left on right side rows and from left to right on wrong side rows. Work football design with yarn A using intarsia method – do not pass yarn across back of work as this distorts image. Use separate lengths of contrast yarn for coloured area and twist yarns together on wrong side when changing colour to avoid holes. Always dec or inc using fully-fashioned method (i.e. on 3rd st from row edge).

Back

With MC and 3 mm (no. 11/US 2) needles, cast on 73 (81; 89) sts. Work 5 cm in ms st. Change to 3.25 mm (no. 10/US 3) needles. Cont in st st until Back measures 21 (26; 31) cm from cast-on edge.

Shape armholes

Cast off 5 (5; 6) sts at beg of next 2 rows.
Cont in st st for 31 (31; 33) cm.

Shape shoulders

Cast off 19 (20; 22) sts at each end of next row to shape shoulders. Place rem 25 (31; 33) sts across centre on stitch holder for neckband. Back should measure 52 (57; 64) cm.

Front

Work as for Back until Front measures 8 (14; 19) cm, ending with a k row.
Next row p 20 (24; 28) with MC, p across 1st row of chart, p 20 (24; 28) with MC.
Next row k 20 (24; 28) with MC, k across 2nd row of chart, k 20 (24; 28) with MC.
Cont as set until Front measures 21 (26; 31) cm.

Shape armholes

Cast off 5 (5; 6) sts at beg of next 2 rows.
Cont working as set until chart is completed.
Cont in st st until Front measures 44 (48; 55) cm from cast-on edge.

Shape neck

Next row cont in st st, work 29 (30; 32) sts, turn. Work on this set of sts only. Cont in st st, but dec 1 st at neck edge on next 7 rows, then on foll 3 alt rows. Cont in st st until Front measures 52 (57; 64) cm from cast-on edge. Cast off rem 19 (20; 22) sts to shape shoulder. With right side facing, place centre 11 (11; 13) sts on stitch holder for neckband, rejoin yarn to rem 29 (30; 32) sts and cont in st st to end. Rep neck shaping for opposite side to match.

Sleeves

With MC and 3.25 mm (no. 10/US 3) needles, cast on 38 (40; 42) sts. Work 5 cm in ms st. Change to 4 mm (no. 8/US 6) needles. Cont in st st, but inc 1 st at each end of next row, then every foll 7th row 7 (9; 11) times. Cont in st st until Sleeve measures 22 (30; 35) cm from cast-on edge. Cast off.

Neck

Sew right shoulder seam. With MC and 3 mm (no. 11/US 2) needles, pick up sts around neck edge. Pick up all 25 (31; 33) sts from Back and all 11 (11; 13) sts from Front reserved on stitch holders for neckband, but miss every 4th st on either side of Front neck edge. Work 3 cm in k1, p1 rib, then 6 rows in st st. Cast off evenly but not too tightly. The st st rows will roll to front.

Making Up

Sew left shoulder seam and side of neckband. Sew in sleeves, joining cast-off edges of sleeves to vertical edges of body. When sewing in sleeves, attach top 2 cm of side seams to 5 (5; 6) cast off sts on body. Sew side seams of body. Only sew side seam to just above ms st hem leaving a side split. Sew sleeve seams. Use mattress stitch or a neat backstitch – do not use overstitch.

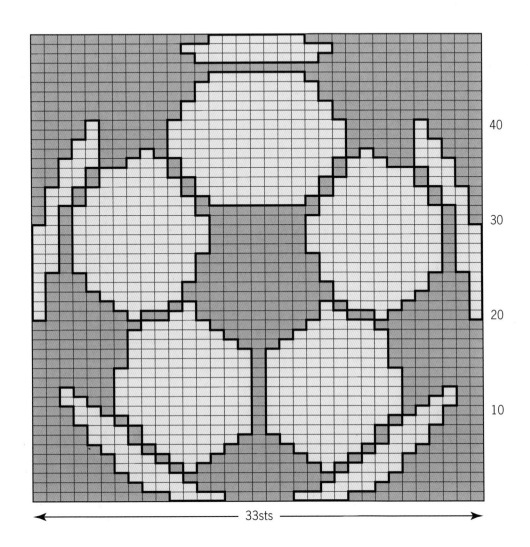

33sts

Key

■ navy (MC)

□ ecru (A)

Star sweater

See picture on page 39

<u>Size</u> To fit age 2–4 years; 4–6 years
<u>Yarn</u> 7 (8) x 50 g balls of Rowan Handknit DK Cotton in navy (MC) and 1 x 50 g ball of Rowan Handknit DK Cotton in ecru (A)
<u>Needles</u> 1 pair each of 3.25 mm (no. 10/US 3) and 4 mm (no. 8/US 6)
<u>Tension</u> 20 sts and 28 rows to 10 cm square over st st on 4 mm (no. 8/US 6) needles. Always work a tension swatch and change needles accordingly if necessary (see Basic Information, page 54).

<u>Ability</u> 3
<u>Abbreviations</u> see Basic Information, pages 54–6.
<u>Note</u> Read chart from right to left on right side rows and from left to right on wrong side rows. Work star design with yarn A using intarsia method – do not pass yarn across back of work as this distorts image. Use separate lengths of contrast yarn for coloured area and twist yarns together on wrong side when changing colour to avoid holes. Always dec or inc using fully-fashioned method (i.e. on 3rd st from row edge).

Back
With yarn A and 3.25 mm (no. 10/US 3) needles, cast on 73 (81) sts. Change to MC. K 4 rows. Change to 4 mm (no. 8/US 6) needles. Beg with a k row, work 66 (72) rows in st st.

Shape armholes
Cast off 4 (5) sts at beg next 2 rows. Work 38 (44) rows in st st.

Shape shoulders
Cast off 18 (19) sts at each end on next row to shape shoulders. Place rem 29 (33) sts across centre on stitch holder for neckband.

Front
Work as for Back until 21 (33) rows of st st have been completed.
Next row p 17 (21) with MC, p across 1st row of chart, p 17 (21) with MC.
Next row k 17 (21) with MC, k across 2nd row of chart, k 17 (21) with MC.
Cont as set until 45th (39th) row of chart has been worked.

Shape armholes
Cont working from chart, but cast off 4 (5) sts at beg of next 2 rows. Cont as set until chart has been completed. Work 12 (11) rows in st st.

Shape neck
For size 2–4 years
Next row k 24, turn.
Work on this set of sts only. Cont in st st, but dec 1 st at neck edge on next row, then on foll 2 alt rows. Rep last 5 rows. Work 5 rows in st st. Cast off rem 18 sts for shoulder. With right side facing, slip centre 17 (15) sts on stitch holder for neckband, rejoin yarn to rem 24 (28) sts and k to end. Rep neck shaping for opposite side to match.

For size 4–6 years
Next row p (28), turn.
Work on this set of sts only. Cont in st st, but dec 1 st at neck edge on next 7 rows, then on foll 2 alt rows. Work 5 rows in st st. Cast off rem 19 sts for shoulder. With wrong side facing, slip centre 17 (15) sts on stitch holder for neckband, rejoin yarn to rem 28 sts and p to end. Rep neck shaping for opposite side to match.

Sleeves
With 3.25 mm (no. 10/US 3) needles and yarn A, cast on 40 (42) sts. Change to MC. K 8 rows. Change to 4 mm (no. 8/US 3) needles. Cont in st st, but inc 1 st at each end of next row and every foll 6th row until 60 (64) sts. Cont in st st until Sleeve measures 30 (35) cm. Cast off.

Neck
Sew right shoulder seam. With MC and 3.25 mm (no. 10/US 3) needles, pick up sts around neck edge. Pick up all 29 (33) sts across Back and all 17 (15) sts across Front, but missing every 4th st either side of Front neck edge. K 5 rows. Change to yarn A. With rs facing, k 1 row. Cast off evenly purlwise, but not too tightly.

Making Up
Sew left shoulder seam. Sew in sleeves, joining cast-off edges of sleeves to vertical edges of body. When sewing in sleeves, attach top 2 cm of side seams to 4 (5) cast off sts on body. Sew side seams of body. Sew sleeve seams. Use mattress stitch or a neat backstitch – do not use overstitch.

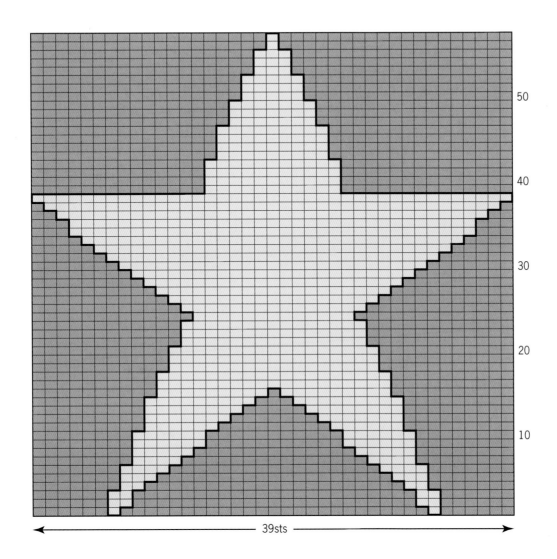

50

40

30

20

10

← 39sts →

Key

navy (MC)

ecru (A)

Popeye sweater

See picture on page 41

Size To fit age 2–4 years; 4–6 years

Yarn 7 (8) x 50 g balls of Rowan Handknit DK Cotton in navy (MC) and 1 x 50 g ball each of Dyed in the Wool Cotton Chenille in cream (A) and gold (B)

Needles 1 pair each of 3.25 mm (no. 10/US 3) and 4 mm (no. 8/US 6)

Tension 20 sts and 28 rows to 10 cm square over st st on 4 mm (no. 8/US 6) needles. Always work a tension swatch and change needles accordingly if necessary (see Basic Information, page 54).

Ability 4

Abbreviations See Basic Information, pages 54–6.

Note Read chart from right to left on right side rows and from left to right on wrong side rows. Work anchor design with yarns A and B using intarsia method – do not pass yarn across back of work as this distorts image. Use separate lengths of contrast yarn for coloured area and twist yarns together on wrong side when changing colour to avoid holes. Always dec or inc using the fully-fashioned method (i.e. on 3rd st from row edge).

Back

With MC and 3.25 mm (no. 10/US 3) needles, cast on 73 (81) sts. Work 12 (16) rows in ms st. Change to 4 mm (no. 8/US 6) needles.
Beg with a k row, work 62 (80) rows in st st.

Shape armholes

Cast off 4 (5) sts at beg of next 2 rows. Work 38 (44) rows in st st.

Shape shoulders

Cast off 18 sts at each end of next row to shape shoulders. Place rem 29 (35) sts across centre on stitch holder for neckband.

Front

Work as for Back until 8 (24) rows of st st have been completed.

Next row k 17 (21) with MC, k across 1st row of chart, k 17 (21) with MC.

Next row p 17 (21) with MC, p across 2nd row of chart, p 17 (21) with MC.

Cont as set until 54th (56th) row of chart has been worked.

Shape armholes

For size 2–4 years

Cont working from chart, but cast off 4 sts at beg of next 2 rows. Cont as set until chart has been completed. Work 26 rows in st st.

For size 4–6 years

Cast off 5 sts at beg of next 2 rows. Work 20 rows in st st.

Shape neck

Next row k 27, turn.

Work on this set of sts only. Cont in st st, but dec 1 st at neck edge on next 6 (4) rows, then on foll 3 (5) alt rows. Work 5 rows in st st. Cast off rem 18 sts for shoulder. With rs facing, slip centre 11 (17) sts on stitch holder for neckband, rejoin yarn to rem 27 sts and k to end. Rep neck shaping for opposite side to match.

Sleeves

With yarn A and 3.25 mm (no. 10/US 3) needles, cast on 40 (42) sts. Change to MC. Work 10 rows in ms st. Change to 4 mm (no. 8/US 3) needles. Cont in st st, but inc 1 st at each end on next row, then every foll 6th row until 60 (64) sts. Cont in st st until Sleeve measures 30 (35) cm. Cast off.

Neckband

Sew right shoulder seam. With MC and 3.25 mm (no. 10/US 3) needles, pick up sts around neck edge. Pick up all 29 (35) sts from Back and all 11 (17) sts from Front reserved on stitch holders for neckband, but miss every 4th st on either side of Front neck edge. Work 2.5 cm in k1, p1 rib. Cast off evenly but not too tightly.

Making Up

Sew left shoulder seam. Sew in sleeves, joining cast-off edges of sleeves to vertical edges of body. Sew side seams of body. Only sew side seam to just above ms st hem leaving a side split. Sew sleeve seams. Use mattress stitch or a neat backstitch – do not use overstitch.

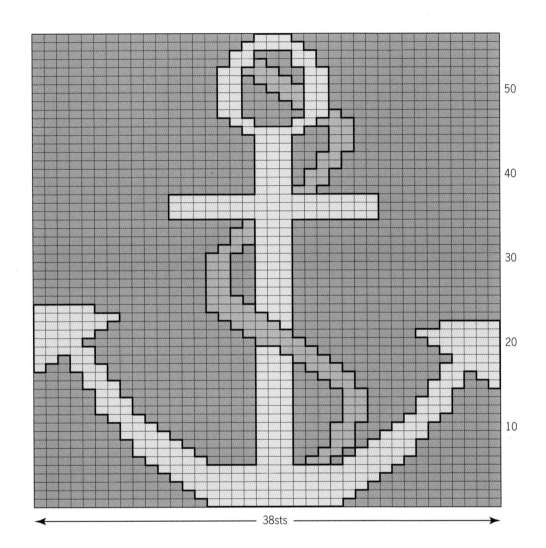

38sts

Key

navy (MC)

cream (A)

gold (B)

Sherlock hat

See picture on page 43

<u>Size</u> To fit age 0–6 months; 6 months–2 years; 2–4 years

<u>Yarn</u> 2 (2; 2) x 50 g balls of Jaeger Siena in cream (MC) and
1 (1; 1) x 50 g ball of Jaeger Siena in navy (A)

<u>Hook</u> 2 mm

<u>Tension</u> 12 sts to 2.5 cm on 2 mm hook. Always work a tension swatch and change hook accordingly if necessary.

<u>Ability</u> 2

<u>Abbreviations</u> See Basic Information, pages 54–6.

Hat

With MC and 2 mm hook, make chain of 6 sts. Join into ring with sl st.

Round 1 12 dc into loop. Join with sl st.

Round 2 1 ch, * 1 dc in next st, 2 dc in next st *, rep from * to * to end.

Round 3 1 ch, ** 1 dc in each of next 2 sts, 2 dc in next st **, rep from ** to ** to end.

Round 4 work as round 3 but inc on every 4th st. Cont inc as set until round 17 (19; 22). Cont in circular method (ie. with no seams), working 1 dc into each dc for 27 (30; 33) rounds.

Earflap

At sides of work, work 16 (17; 18) dc, turn.

Next row work 1 dc into each dc to end. Rep last 2 rows twice.

Next row dec 1 st at each end of next row and every foll row until 4 sts. Work second earflap. Beg on 42nd (44th; 46th) st from last st of first earflap. Work second earflap as first.

Finishing

With yarn A, work 2 rounds in dc around edge of hat.

Make loop

With yarn A, put hook through top of hat and make 10 ch. Join last ch to first. Make 22 dc into chain loop. Fasten off.

Make ties

With yarn A used double, put hook through st at bottom centre of earflap and make chain approx 20 cm long. Fasten off.

Zig-zag sweater

See picture on page 45

<u>Size</u> To fit age 2–4 years; 4–6 years

<u>Yarn</u> 8 (10) x 50 g balls of Rowan Handknit DK Cotton

<u>Needles</u> 1 pair each of 3.25 mm (no. 10/US 3) and 4 mm (no. 8/US 6), and cable needle

<u>Tension</u> 20 sts and 28 rows to 10 cm square over st st on 4 mm (no. 8/US 6) needles. Always work a tension swatch and change needles accordingly if necessary (see Basic Information, page 54).

<u>Ability</u> 2

<u>Abbreviations</u> See Basic Information, pages 54–6.

c5f = sl next 3 sts on cn and leave at front of work, k2, then k3 from cn

<u>Note</u> Read chart from right to left on right side rows and from left to right on wrong side rows. Always dec or inc using fully-fashioned method (i.e. on 3rd st from row edge).

Back

With 3.25 mm (no. 10/US 3) needles, cast on 79 (87) sts. Work 3 cm in ms st. Change to 4 mm (no. 8/US 6) needles.

Work moss stitch and cable pattern

Rows 1, 5 and 7 work 9 (6) sts in ms st, [k 5, work 9 sts in ms st] 4 (5) times, k 5, work 9 (6) sts in ms st.

Rows 2, 4, 6 and 8 work 9 (6) sts in ms st, [p 5, work 9 sts in ms st] 4 (5) times, p 5, work 9 (6) sts in ms st.

Rows 3 and 9 work 9 (6) sts in ms st, [c5f, work 9 sts in ms st] 4 (5) times, c5f, work 9 (6) sts in ms st.

Rep last 6 rows a further 10 (12) times.

Next row work 9 sts (6) sts in ms st, [p 5, work 9 sts in ms st] 4 (5) times, p 5, work 9 (6) sts in ms st.

For size 2–4 years

Next row work 9 sts in ms st, [k 5, work 9 sts in ms st] 5 times.

Next row work 9 sts in ms st, [p 5, work 9 sts in ms st] 5 times.

Work zig-zag pattern

Next row work across 1st row of chart A, but rep centre 14 sts 5 (6) times.

Next row work across 2nd row of chart A, but rep centre 14 sts 5 (6) times.

Cont in patt as set until chart is completed. Work 4 rows in st st. K 4 rows. Work 4 rows in st st.

Work zig-zag pattern

Next row work across 1st row of chart B, but rep centre 14 sts 5 (6) times.

Next row work across 2nd row of chart B, but rep centre 14 sts 5 (6) times.

Cont in patt as set until chart is completed. Work 4 rows in st st. K 4 rows. Work 4 rows in st st.

Shape shoulders

Cast off 24 (27) sts at each end of next row to shape shoulders. Place rem 31 (33) sts across centre on stitch holder for neckband.

Front

Work as for Back until 5th (6th) row of chart B has been worked.

Shape neck

For size 2–4 years

Next row work 33 sts across 6th row of chart B, turn.

Work on this set of sts only. Cont in patt as set, but dec 1 st at neck edge on next 4 rows and foll alt row. Work 4 rows in st st, but dec 1 st at neck edge on foll 2 alt rows. Work 4 rows in gt st, but dec 1 st at neck edge on foll 2 alt rows.

For size 4–6 years

Next row work 37 sts across 7th row of chart B, turn.

Work on this set of sts only. Cont in patt as set, but dec 1 st at neck edge on next 5 rows. Work 4 rows in st st, but dec 1 st at neck edge on next 3 rows. Work 4 rows in gt st, but dec 1 st at neck edge on next row and foll alt row. Cast off rem 24 (27) sts for shoulder. With rs facing, place centre 13 sts on stitch holder for neckband, rejoin yarn to rem 33 (37) sts

and cont in patt to end. Rep patterning and neck shaping for opposite side to match.

Sleeves

With 3.25 mm (no. 10/US 3) needles, cast on 40 sts. Work 3 cm in ms st. Change to 4 mm (no. 8/US 6) needles. Cont in ms st, but inc 1 st at each end of next row and every foll 7th row until 60 (64) sts. Cont in ms st until Sleeve measures 23 (28) cm from cast-on edge. Cast off.

Neck

Sew right shoulder seam. With 3.25 mm (no. 10/US 3) needles, pick up sts around neck edge. Pick up all 31 (33) sts across Back and all 13 sts across Front reserved on stitch holders for neckband, but missing every 4th st either side of Front neck edge. Work 3 cm in k2, p2 rib. Cast off evenly in rib but not too tightly.

Making Up

Sew left shoulder seam. Sew in sleeves, joining cast-off edges of sleeves to vertical edges of body with neat backstitch 15 (17) cm below shoulder seam. When sewing in sleeves, attach top 2 cm of side seams to 4 (5) cast-off sts on body. Sew side seams of body. Only sew side seams to just above ms st hem leaving a side split. Sew sleeve seams. Use mattress stitch or a neat backstitch – do not use overstitch.

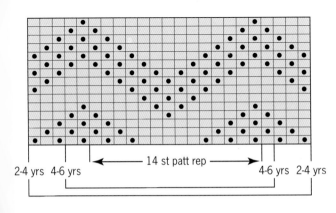

2-4 yrs 4-6 yrs ← 14 st patt rep → 4-6 yrs 2-4 yrs

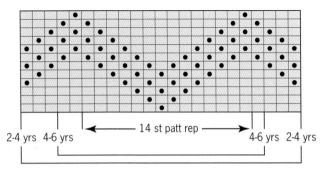

2-4 yrs 4-6 yrs ← 14 st patt rep → 4-6 yrs 2-4 yrs

Chart A   **Chart B**   **Key**

☐ k on rs row, p on ws row

⦿ p on rs row, k on ws row

Star jacket

See picture on pages 46–7

Size To fit age 2–4 years; 4–6 years
Yarn 7 (8) x 50 g balls of Rowan Handknit DK Cotton
in plum (MC) and 1 (1) x 50 g ball each of Rowan
Handknit DK Cotton in gold (A) and green (B)
Needles 1 pair each of 3.25 mm (no. 10/US 3) and 4
mm (no. 8/US 6)
Tension 20 sts and 28 rows to 10 cm square over st st
on 4 mm (no. 8/US 6) needles. Always work a tension
swatch and change needles accordingly if
necessary (see Basic Information, page 54).

Ability 4
Abbreviations See Basic Information, pages 54–6.
Note Read chart from right to left on right side rows
and from left to right on wrong side rows. Work star
design with yarn B using intarsia method – do not
pass yarn across back of work as this distorts
image. Use separate lengths of contrast yarn for
coloured area and twist yarns together on wrong
side when changing colour to avoid holes. Always
dec or inc using fully-fashioned method (i.e. on 3rd
st from row edge).

Back

With yarn A and 3.25 mm (no. 10/US 3)
needles, cast on 73 (81) sts. K 8 rows.
Change to MC and 4 mm (no. 8/US 6) needles.
Beg with a k row, work 44 rows in st st.
Next row k 20 (24) with MC, k across 1st row
of chart, k 20 (24) with MC.
Next row p 20 (24), p across 1st row of chart,
p 20 (24) with MC.
Cont as set until 24th row of chart has been
worked.

Shape armholes

Cont working from chart, but cast off 5 (5) sts
at beg of next 2 rows. Cont as set until chart
has been completed. Work 14 (22) rows in
st st.

Shape shoulders

Cast off 19 (20) sts at each end on next row to
shape shoulders. Place rem 25 (31) sts across
centre on stitch holder for neckband.

Pocket Bags

With MC and 3.25 mm (no. 10/US 3) needles,
cast on 20 sts. Work 26 rows in st st. Place
20 sts on stitch holder. Work 2 pocket bags.

Left Front

With yarn A and 3.25 mm (no. 10/US 3)
needles, cast on 32 (36) sts. K 8 rows. Change
to yarn B and 4 mm (no. 8/US 6) needles. Beg
with a k row, work 26 rows in st st.

Add pocket bags

Next row k 6 (10) sts, place next 20 sts on stitch
holder for pocket bands, k 20 sts reserved on
stitch holder for pocket bags, k to end.
Work 40 (41) rows in st st.

Shape armholes

Cast off 5 sts at end (beg) of next row. Work 23
(28) rows in st st.

Shape neck

Cont in st st, but dec 2 (3) sts at beg of next
row, dec 1 st at neck edge of next 3 (4) rows
and dec 1 st at neck edge of foll 4 (5) alt rows.
Work 2 rows in st st. Cast off rem 19 sts for
shoulders.

Right Front

Work as for Left Front but rev all patterning
and shaping.

Sleeves

With yarn A and 3.25 mm (no. 10/US 3)
needles, cast on 40 sts. K 8 rows. Change to
MC and 4 mm (no. 8/US 3) needles. Cont in st
st, but inc 1 st at each end of next row and
every foll 8th row until 52 (62) sts. Cont in st st
until Sleeve measures 28 (34) cm. Cast off.

Making Up

Sew shoulder seams. Sew in sleeves, joining
cast-off edge of sleeves to vertical edges of
body. When sewing in sleeves, attach top 2 cm
of side seams to 4 (5) cast off sts on body.
Sew side seams of body. Sew sleeve seams.
Use mattress stitch or a neat backstitch – do
not use overstitch.

Pocket Bands

With yarn B and 3.25 mm (no. 10/US 3)
needles, pick up 20 sts reserved on stitch
holder for pocket bands. K 6 rows. Cast off.
Sew pocket bags neatly to inside of jacket.

Left Front Band

With yarn A and 3.25 mm (no. 10/US 3)
needles, cast on 8 sts. Work in gt st until band
measures from hem to neck shaping of Left
Front when slightly stretched.

Right Front Band

With yarn A and 3.25 mm (no. 10/US 3)
needles, cast on 8 sts. K 8 rows.

Make buttonhole

Next row k 5, cast off next 2 sts, k to end.
Next row k 1, cast on 2 sts over those cast off
in previous row, k to end.
Cont in gt st, but make a further 5 buttonholes
every 4 (5) cm. Cont in gt st until band
measures from hem to neck shaping of Right
Front when slightly stretched. Sew button
bands to jacket with mattress stitch or neat
flat stitch – do not use overstitch.

Neck and Collar

With MC and 3.25 mm (no. 10/US 3) needles,
cast on 6 sts. K 1 row. Cont in gt st, but inc 1 st
at each end of next row and every foll alt row
until 12 sts. K 1 row. Cont in gt st, but inc 1 st
at beg of next row and every foll alt row until
26 sts. K 52 (62) rows. Cont in gt st, but dec 1
st at end of next row and every foll alt row
until 12 sts. K 1 row. Cont in gt st, but dec 1 st
at each end of next row and every foll alt row
until 6 sts. K 1 row. Cast off. Pin collar into
position and sew into place. Pass needle
through ridge on either side of work to form a
neat flat seam. Join cast-on edge and cast-off
edge to front at neck edge beg halfway across
button band.

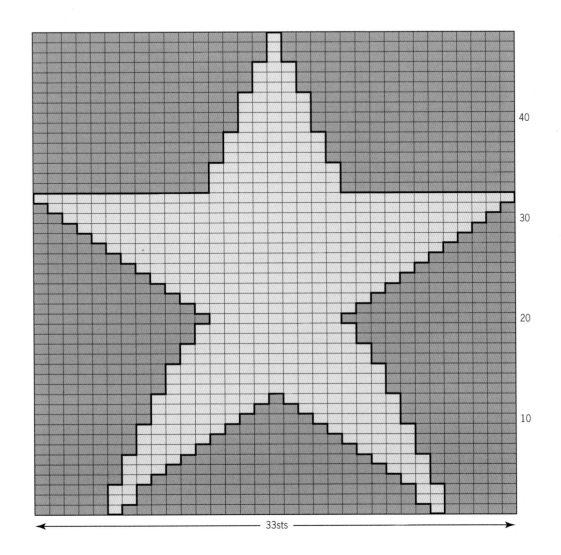

40

30

20

10

← 33sts →

Key

■ navy (MC)

□ gold (A)

Heart and Star scarves

See pictures on pages 48–9

Size One size (approximately 80 cm long)

Yarn 3 x 50 g balls Rowan Handknit DK Cotton in pink for Heart hat or navy for Star hat (MC) and 1 x 50 g ball **Dyed in the** Wool Cotton Chenille in cherry for Heart hat or Rowan Handknit DK Cotton in ecru for Star hat (A)

Needles 1 pair each of 3.25 mm (no. 10/US 3) and 4 mm (no. 8/US 6)

Tension 20 sts and 28 rows to 10 cm square over st st on 4 mm (no. 8/US 6) needles. Always work a tension swatch and change needles accordingly if necessary (see Basic Information, pages 54).

Ability 1

Abbreviations See Basic Information, pages 54–6.

Note Read chart from right to left on right side rows and from left to right on wrong side rows. Work heart or star design with yarn A using intarsia method – do not pass yarn across back of work as this distorts image. Use separate lengths of contrast yarn for coloured area and twist yarns together on wrong side when changing colour to avoid holes.

Scarf

With MC and 4 mm (no. 8/US 6) needles, cast on 30 sts. K 12 rows.

Next row k to end.

Next row k7, p to last 7 sts, k to end.

Rep last 2 rows until work measures 18 cm, ending with a p row.

Next row k 15, turn.

Work on this set of sts only. Cont as set on 15 sts until work measures 24 cm, ending with a p row. Place these 15 sts on stitch holder. Rejoin yarn to rem 15 sts and rep on opposite side to match. With rs facing, rejoin yarn to 15 sts kept on stitch holder for rs of scarf, then k all 30 sts to rejoin 2 halves. Cont as set until Scarf measures 28 cm, ending with a p row.

For heart design

Next row k9 with MC, k across 1st row of chart A, k8 with MC.

Next row p8 with MC, p across 2nd row of chart A, p9 with MC.

For star design

Next row k9 with MC, k across 1st row of chart B, k8 with MC.

Next row p8 with MC, p across 2nd row of chart B, p9 with MC.

Cont as set until 16th row of chart has been worked. Work a further 4 cm in st st with gt st borders. K 12 rows. Cast off.

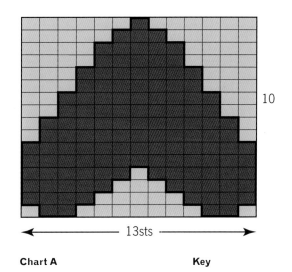

10

Chart A

Key

☐ pink (MC)

▨ cherry (A)

13sts

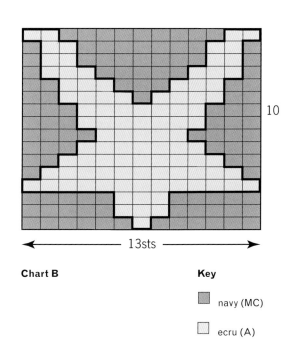

10

Chart B

Key

▨ navy (MC)

☐ ecru (A)

13sts

Heart and Star hats

See pictures on pages 48–9

<u>Size</u> To fit age 6–12 months; 1–3 years; 3–6 years
<u>Yarn</u> 1 (1; 1) x 50 g ball Rowan Handknit **DK** Cotton in pink for Heart hat or navy for Star hat (**MC**) and 1 (1; 1) x 50 g ball Dyed in the Wool Cotton Chenille in cherry for Heart hat or Rowan Handknit **DK** Cotton in ecru for Star hat (**A**)
<u>Needles</u> 1 pair each of 3.25 mm (no. 10/**US** 3) and 4 mm (no. 8/**US** 6)
<u>Tension</u> 20 sts and 28 rows to 10 cm square over st st on 4 mm (no. 8/**US** 6) needles. Always work a tension swatch and change needles accordingly if necessary

(see Basic Information, page 54).
<u>Ability</u> 2
<u>Abbreviations</u> See Basic Information, pages 54–6.
<u>Note</u> Read chart from right to left on right side rows and from left to right on wrong side rows. Work heart or star design with yarn A using intarsia method – do not pass yarn across back of work as this distorts image. Use separate lengths of contrast yarn for coloured area and twist yarns together on wrong side when changing colour to avoid holes. Always dec or inc using fully-fashioned method (i.e. on 3rd stitch from row edge).

Hat

With MC and 3.25 mm (no. 10/US 3) needles, cast on 79 (91; 103) sts. K 8 rows.
Change to 4 mm (no. 8/US 6) needles.
K 1 row.

For heart design

Next row p33 (39; 45) with MC, p across 1st row of chart A, p33 (39; 45) with MC.
Next row k33 (39; 45) with MC, k across 1st row of chart A, k33 (39; 45) with MC.

For star design

Next row p33 (39; 45) with MC, p across 1st row of chart B, p33 (39; 45) with MC.
Next row k33 (39; 45) with MC, k across 1st row of chart B, k33 (39; 45) with MC.
Cont working as set until 16th row of chart has been worked. P 1 row.
Next row * k11 (13; 15), k2tog **, rep from * to ** to last st, k1.
Next row p to end

Next row * k10 (12; 14), k2tog **, rep from * to ** to last st, k1.
Next row p to end
Cont as set until 19 (25; 25) sts.

Making Up

Thread yarn end twice through rem sts and pull up tight. Sew seam with mattress stitch or neat backstitch – do not use overstitch.

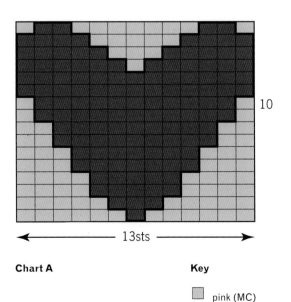

10

← — 13sts — →

Chart A

Key

  pink (MC)

  cherry (A)

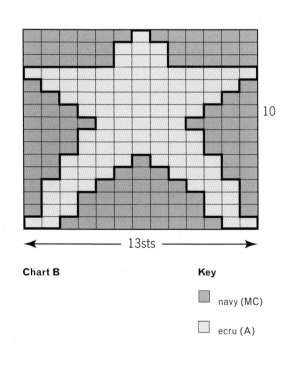

10

← — 13sts — →

Chart B

Key

  navy (MC)

  ecru (A)

Heart and Star rucksacks

See pictures on page 51

<u>Size</u> One size (approximately 24 cm x 22.5 cm)

<u>Yarn</u> 2 x 50 g balls Rowan Handknit DK Cotton in pink for Heart rucksack or navy for Star rucksack (MC) and 1 x 50 g ball Dyed in the Wool Cotton Chenille in cherry for Heart rucksack or Rowan Handknit DK Cotton in ecru for Star rucksack (A)

<u>Needles</u> 1 pair each of 3.25 mm (no. 10/US 3) and 4 mm (no. 8/US 6)

<u>Tension</u> 20 sts and 28 rows to 10 cm square over st st on 4 mm (no. 8/US 6) needles. Always work a tension swatch and change needles accordingly if necessary (see Basic Information, pages 54).

<u>Ability</u> 2

<u>Abbreviations</u> See Basic Information, pages 54–6.

<u>Note</u> Read chart from right to left on right side rows and from left to right on wrong side rows. Work heart or star design with yarn A using intarsia method – do not pass yarn across back of work as this distorts image. Use separate lengths of contrast yarn for coloured area and twist yarns together on wrong side when changing colour to avoid holes.

Rucksack

With MC and 3.25 mm (no. 10/US 3) needles, cast on 45 sts. Work 16 rows in st st. Place marker at each end of last row to indicate where channel for cord ends or k next row tog with cast-on edge to form channel. Change to 4 mm (no. 8/US 6) needles. Work 60 rows in st st. Place marker at each end of this row to indicate fold. Work 15 rows in st st.

For heart design

Next row k13 with MC, k across 1st row of chart A, k13 with MC.

Next row p13 with MC, p across 2nd row of chart A, p12 with MC.

Cont as set until 32nd row of chart has been worked. Work 13 rows in st st.

For star design

Next row k12 with MC, k across 1st row of chart B, k12 with MC.

Next row p12 with MC, p across 2nd row of chart B, p12 with MC.

Cont as set until 30th row of chart has been worked. Work 15 rows in st st.

Place marker at each end of last row to indicate channel for cord. Change to 3.25 mm (no. 10/US 3) needles. Work 16 rows in st st. Cast off tog with marked row to make channel.

Making Up

Sew side seams folding rucksack in half where marked. Sew to channel only.

Strap

With MC and 3.25 mm (no. 10/US 3) needles, pick up 8 sts from bottom right-hand folded edge. Work 106 cm in st st. Thread strap through channel beg on right side at back, through front channel and then through back again. Strap should come out on left side. Sew end neatly and securely to bottom left-hand corner.

Chart A

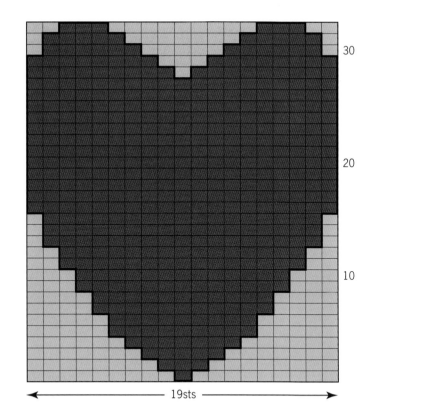

30

20

10

← 19sts →

Key

■ pink (MC)

■ cherry (A)

Chart B

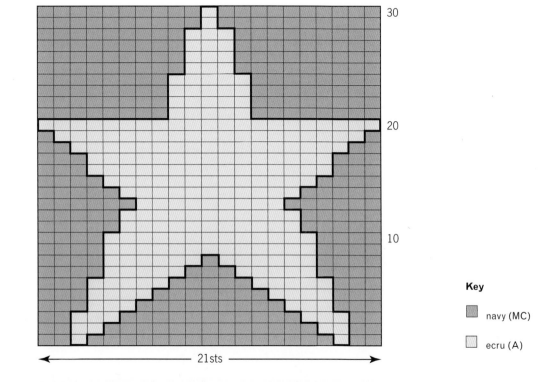

30

20

10

← 21sts →

Key

■ navy (MC)

☐ ecru (A)

Stockists and suppliers

Little Badger
A range of yarn and ready-to-wear garments are available by mail order from Little Badger, including knitted sweaters, cardigans, jackets, dresses, blankets, bags, hats and scarves, printed t-shirts and silk dresses, cushions and blankets. For a catalogue or to place an order please contact Little Badger at the address given below.

Little Badger
6 Macaulay Road
London SW4 0QX
tel: +44 (0) 20 7498 4707
fax: +44 (0) 20 7498 4707
email: littlebadger@btconnect.com
http: www.littlebadger.com

Dyed in the Wool
A range of yarns are available by mail order from Dyed in the Wool at the address given below.

Dyed in the Wool
The Sidings Industrial Estate
Settle
North Yorkshire BD24 9RP
tel: +44 (0) 1729 822106
fax: +44 (0) 1729 822750
email: rider@dyedinthewool.co.uk
http: www.dyedinthewool.co.uk

Jaeger Handknits
Jaeger yarns are widely available in yarn shops. For details of stockists and mail order sources for Jaeger yarns please contact the distributors listed below.

Canada
Diamond Yarns
9697 St Laurent
Montreal
Quebec H3L 2N1
tel: +1 (514) 388 6188

Diamond Yarns
155 Martin Ross
Unit 3
Toronto
Ontario M3J 2L9
tel: +1 (416) 736 6111

China
c/o East Unity Company Ltd
Rm 902
Block A
Kailey Industrial Centre
12 Fung Yip Street
Chai Wan
tel: +86 (2869) 7110

Denmark
Ruzicka
Hydesbyvei 27
DK 4990
Sakskobing
tel: +45 (54) 70 78 03

Finland
Coats Molnlycke Ompelulanka
Ketjutie 3
FIN 04220
Kerava
tel: +358 (9) 274871

Holland
de Afstap
Oude Leliestraat 12
1015 AW Amsterdam
tel: +31 (20) 6231445

Hong Kong
East Unity Company Ltd
Rm 902
Block A
Kailey Industrial Centre
12 Fung Yip Street
Chai Wan
tel: +852 2869 7110

Iceland
Storkurinn
Kjorgardi
Laugavegi 59
ICE-101 Reykjavik
tel: +354 551 82 58

Japan
Puppy Company Ltd
TOC Building
7-22 17 Nishigotanda
Shinagawa-ku
Tokyo
tel: +81 (3) 3494 2395

Sweden
c/o Ruzicka
Hydesbyvei 27
DK 4990
Sakskobing
Denmark
tel: +45 (54) 70 78 04

Taiwan
Green Leave Company Ltd
PO Box 11183 Taipei
No 24 Yong Shing Street
Jong-Hor
Taipei
tel: +886 (2) 974 1035

United Kingdom
Green Lane Mill
Holmfirth
West Yorkshire HD7 1RW
tel: +44 (0) 1484 680050 / 681881

United States of America
Knitting Fever Inc
PO Box 52
35 Debevoise Avenue
Roosevelt
New York 11575-0502
tel: +1 (516) 546 3600

Rowan Yarns
Rowan yarns are widely available in yarn shops. For details of stockists and mail order sources for Rowan yarns please contact the distributors listed under Jaeger Handknits, unless an alternative address for that particular country is listed below.

Australia
Sunspun
185 Canterbury Road
Canterbury 3126
tel: +61 (3) 5979 1555

Belgium
Pavan
Koningin Astridlaan 78
B9000 Gent
tel: +32 (9) 221 8591

France
Elle Tricot
4 rue de Paques
67000 Strasbourg
tel: +33 (3) 88 23 03 13

Germany
Wolle & Design
Wolfshoverstraße 76
52428 Julich-Stetternich
tel: +49 (2461) 54735

Japan
DiaKeito Company Ltd
2-3-11 Senba-Higashi
Minoh City
Osaka
tel: +81 (6) 27 27 6604

Norway
c/o Ruzicka
Hydesbyvei 27
DK 4990
Sakskobing
Denmark
tel: +45 (54) 70 78 04

Sweden
Wincent
Norrtulsgaten 65
11345 Stockholm
tel: +46 (8) 673 70 60

United Kingdom
Green Lane Mill
Holmfirth
West Yorkshire HD7 1RW
tel: +44 (0) 1484 681881

United States of America
Westminster Fibres Inc
5 Northern Boulevard
Amherst NH 03031
tel: +1 (603) 886 5041 / 5043

Acknowledgments

Elaine and I would like to thank everyone involved with Little Badger, but especially the following:

Vanessa Aitchison our fantastic assistant who is always inspiring; Ben Murphy for the wonderful photographs and his eagle-eyed attention to detail; Lawrence Morton for designing a very unique knitting book; Matilda, Martha, Ceidra and Freya for being our muses; Graeme Glen for being himself; Atom, Billie, Ceidra, Dexter, Elsa, Finlay, Harry, Iris, Martha, Taylor and their mums and dads for letting us take their pictures; all the fantastic knitters who made the samples but especially Monica McMillan, who continues to surprise us with her ingenuity and quality, Ruth Badger, Suzan Felton, Wray Edmans, Irene Brook, Mrs Stainforth, Pat Cooper and Helen Dawson; Rowan Yarn, Jaeger Handknits and Dyed in the Wool for providing most of the yarn; Anthony Calf for his brilliant help with finding locations and everyone at Little Haven, Ichenor for the use of their house; and last but not least our lovely editor Lisa Pendreigh.